The Rosary of Pope Leo XIII

Compiled from The Great Encyclical Letters of Pope Leo XIII
by Brother Hermenegild

Table of Contents

Introduction..4
Supremi Apostolatus Officio..6
Superiore Anno...13
Quod Auctoritate..17
Vi E Ben Noto..23
Octobri Mense 1891...26
Magnae Dei Matris...36
Laetitiae Sanctae..47
Jucunda Semper Expectatione...55
Adjutricem...63
Fidentem Piumque Animum..73
Augustissimae Virginis Mariae..79
Diuturni Temporis..85

Introduction

Pope Leo XIII, who reigned for over a quarter of a century, following the second longest reigning pope in history, Pope Pius IX, has come to be know as the Pope of the Rosary. During his pontificate he wrote twelve wonderful Encyclicals on the Rosary, encouraging Catholics to recite the Rosary with devotion and profit for their souls.

Leo saw the Rosary as a cure for the ills of today. If we follow his advice and recite the Rosary with true devotion, we will see a cure of our own spiritual ills. From curing our own spiritual ills and working to become saints, we can influence those around us to do the same and bring about restoring the world to where it ought to be.

Supremi Apostolatus Officio

To all the Patriarchs, Primates, Archbishops and Bishops of the Catholic World in the Grace and Communion of the Apostolic See.

Venerable Brethren, Health and the Apostolic Benediction.

The supreme Apostolic office which we discharge and the exceedingly difficult condition of these times, daily warn and almost compel Us to watch carefully over the integrity of the Church, the more that the calamities from which she suffers are greater. While, therefore, we endeavour in every way to preserve the rights of the Church and to obviate or repel present or contingent dangers, We constantly seek for help from Heaven - the sole means of effecting anything - that our labours and our care may obtain their wished for object. We deem that there could be no surer and more efficacious means to this end than by religion and piety to obtain the favour of the great Virgin Mary, the Mother of God, the guardian of our peace and the minister to us of heavenly grace, who is placed on the highest summit of power and glory in Heaven, in order that she may bestow the help of her patronage on men who through so many labours and dangers are striving to reach that eternal city. Now that the anniversary, therefore, of manifold and exceedingly great favours obtained by a Christian people through the devotion of the Rosary is at hand, We desire that that same devotion should be offered by the whole Catholic world with the greatest earnestness to the Blessed Virgin, that by her intercession her Divine Son may be appeased and softened in the evils which afflict us. And therefore We determined, Venerable Brethren, to despatch to you these letters in order that, informed of Our designs, your authority and zeal might excite the piety of your people to conform themselves to them.

2. It has always been the habit of Catholics in danger and in troublous times to fly for refuge to Mary, and to seek for peace in her maternal goodness; showing that the Catholic Church has always, and with justice, put all her hope and trust in the Mother of God. And truly the Immaculate Virgin, chosen to be the Mother of God and thereby associated with Him in the work of man's salvation, has a favour and power with her Son greater than any human or angelic creature has ever obtained, or ever can gain. And, as it is her greatest pleasure to grant her help and comfort to those who seek her, it cannot be doubted

that she would deign, and even be anxious, to receive the aspirations of the universal Church.

3. This devotion, so great and so confident, to the august Queen of Heaven, has never shone forth with such brilliancy as when the militant Church of God has seemed to be endangered by the violence of heresy spread abroad, or by an intolerable moral corruption, or by the attacks of powerful enemies. Ancient and modern history and the more sacred annals of the Church bear witness to public and private supplications addressed to the Mother of God, to the help she has granted in return, and to the peace and tranquillity which she had obtained from God. Hence her illustrious titles of helper, consoler, mighty in war, victorious, and peace-giver. And amongst these is specially to be commemorated that familiar title derived from the Rosary by which the signal benefits she has gained for the whole of Christendom have been solemnly perpetuated. There is none among you, venerable brethren, who will not remember how great trouble and grief God's Holy Church suffered from the Albigensian heretics, who sprung from the sect of the later Manicheans, and who filled the South of France and other portions of the Latin world with their pernicious errors, and carrying everywhere the terror of their arms, strove far and wide to rule by massacre and ruin. Our merciful God, as you know, raised up against these most direful enemies a most holy man, the illustrious parent and founder of the Dominican Order. Great in the integrity of his doctrine, in his example of virtue, and by his apostolic labours, he proceeded undauntedly to attack the enemies of the Catholic Church, not by force of arms; but trusting wholly to that devotion which he was the first to institute under the name of the Holy Rosary, which was disseminated through the length and breadth of the earth by him and his pupils. Guided, in fact, by divine inspiration and grace, he foresaw that this devotion, like a most powerful warlike weapon, would be the means of putting the enemy to flight, and of confounding their audacity and mad impiety. Such was indeed its result. Thanks to this new method of prayer-when adopted and properly carried out as instituted by the Holy Father St. Dominic-piety, faith, and union began to return, and the projects and devices of the heretics to fall to pieces. Many wanderers also returned to the way of salvation, and the wrath of the impious was restrained by the arms of those Catholics who had determined to repel their violence.

4. The efficacy and power of this devotion was also wondrously exhibited in the sixteenth century, when the vast forces of the Turks threatened to impose on nearly the whole of Europe the yoke

of superstition and barbarism. At that time the Supreme Pontiff, St. Pius V., after rousing the sentiment of a common defence among all the Christian princes, strove, above all, with the greatest zeal, to obtain for Christendom the favour of the most powerful Mother of God. So noble an example offered to heaven and earth in those times rallied around him all the minds and hearts of the age. And thus Christ's faithful warriors, prepared to sacrifice their life and blood for the salvation of their faith and their country, proceeded undauntedly to meet their foe near the Gulf of Corinth, while those who were unable to take part formed a pious band of supplicants, who called on Mary, and unitedly saluted her again and again in the words of the Rosary, imploring her to grant the victory to their companions engaged in battle. Our Sovereign Lady did grant her aid; for in the naval battle by the Echinades Islands, the Christian fleet gained a magnificent victory, with no great loss to itself, in which the enemy were routed with great slaughter. And it was to preserve the memory of this great boon thus granted, that the same Most Holy Pontiff desired that a feast in honour of Our Lady of Victories should celebrate the anniversary of so memorable a struggle, the feast which Gregory XIII. dedicated under the title of "The Holy Rosary." Similarly, important successes were in the last century gained over the Turks at Temeswar, in Pannonia, and at Corfu; and in both cases these engagements coincided with feasts of the Blessed Virgin and with the conclusion of public devotions of the Rosary. And this led our predecessor, Clement XI., in his gratitude, to decree that the Blessed Mother of God should every year be especially honoured in her Rosary by the whole Church.

5. Since, therefore, it is clearly evident that this form of prayer is particularly pleasing to the Blessed Virgin, and that it is especially suitable as a means of defence for the Church and all Christians, it is in no way wonderful that several others of Our Predecessors have made it their aim to favour and increase its spread by their high recommendations. Thus Urban IV, testified that "every day the Rosary obtained fresh boon for Christianity." Sixtus IV declared that this method of prayer "redounded to the honour of God and the Blessed Virgin, and was well suited to obviate impending dangers;" Leo X that "it was instituted to oppose pernicious heresiarchs and heresies;" while Julius III called it "the glory of the Church." So also St. Pius V., that "with the spread of this devotion the meditations of the faithful have begun to be more inflamed, their prayers more fervent, and they have suddenly become different men; the darkness of heresy has been dissipated, and the light of Catholic faith has broken forth again."

Lastly Gregory XIII in his turn pronounced that "the Rosary had been instituted by St. Dominic to appease the anger of God and to implore the intercession of the Blessed Virgin Mary."

6. Moved by these thoughts and by the examples of Our Predecessors, We have deemed it most opportune for similar reasons to institute solemn prayers and to endeavour by adopting those addressed to the Blessed Virgin in the recital of the Rosary to obtain from her son Jesus Christ a similar aid against present dangers. You have before your eyes, Venerable Brethren, the trials to which the Church is daily exposed; Christian piety, public morality, nay, even faith itself, the supreme good and beginning of all the other virtues, all are daily menaced with the greatest perils.

7. Nor are you only spectators of the difficulty of the situation, but your charity, like Ours, is keenly wounded; for it is one of the most painful and grievous sights to see so many souls, redeemed by the blood of Christ, snatched from salvation by the whirlwind of an age of error, precipitated into the abyss of eternal death. Our need of divine help is as great today as when the great Dominic introduced the use of the Rosary of Mary as a balm for the wounds of his contemporaries.

8. That great saint indeed, divinely enlightened, perceived that no remedy would be more adapted to the evils of his time than that men should return to Christ, who "is the way, the truth, and the life," by frequent meditation on the salvation obtained for Us by Him, and should seek the intercession with God of that Virgin, to whom it is given to destroy all heresies. He therefore so composed the Rosary as to recall the mysteries of our salvation in succession, and the subject of meditation is mingled and, as it were, interlaced with the Angelic salutation and with the prayer addressed to God, the Father of Our Lord Jesus Christ. We, who seek a remedy for similar evils, do not doubt therefore that the prayer introduced by that most blessed man with so much advantage to the Catholic world, will have the greatest effect in removing the calamities of our times also. Not only do We earnestly exhort all Christians to give themselves to the recital of the pious devotion of the Rosary publicly, or privately in their own house and family, and that unceasingly, but we also desire that the whole of the month of October in this year should be consecrated to the Holy Queen of the Rosary. We decree and order that in the whole Catholic world, during this year, the devotion of the Rosary shall be solemnly celebrated by special and splendid services. From the first day of next October, therefore, until the second day of the November following, in every parish and, if the ecclesiastical authority deem it opportune and

of use, in every chapel dedicated to the Blessed Virgin - let five decades of the Rosary be recited with the addition of the Litany of Loreto. We desire that the people should frequent these pious exercises; and We will that either Mass shall be said at the altar, or that the Blessed Sacrament shall be exposed to the adoration of the faithful, Benediction being afterwards given with the Sacred Host to the pious congregation. We highly approve of the confraternities of the Holy Rosary of the Blessed Virgin going in procession, following ancient custom, through the town, as a public demonstration of their devotion. And in those places where this is not possible, let it be replaced by more assiduous visits to the churches, and let the fervour of piety display itself by a still greater diligence in the exercise of the Christian virtues.

9. In favour of those who shall do as We have above laid down, We are pleased to open the heavenly treasure-house of the Church that they may find therein at once encouragements and rewards for their piety. We therefore grant to all those who, in the prescribed space of time, shall have taken part in the public recital of the Rosary and the Litanies, and shall have prayed for Our intention, seven years and seven times forty days of indulgence, obtainable each time. We will that those also shall share in these favours who are hindered by a lawful cause from joining in these public prayers of which We have spoken, provided that they shall have practiced those devotions in private and shall have prayed to God for Our intention. We remit all punishment and penalties for sins committed, in the form of a Pontifical indulgence, to all who, in the prescribed time, either publicly in the churches or privately at home (when hindered from the former by lawful cause) shall have at least twice practiced these pious exercises; and who shall have, after due confession, approached the holy table. We further grant a plenary indulgence to those who, either on the feast of the Blessed Virgin of the Rosary or within its octave, after having similarly purified their souls by a salutary confession, shall have approached the table of Christ and prayed in some church according to Our intention to God and the Blessed Virgin for the necessities of the Church.

10. And you, Venerable Brethren, - the more you have at heart the honour of Mary, and the welfare of human society, the more diligently apply yourselves to nourish the piety of the people towards the great Virgin, and to increase their confidence in her. We believe it to be part of the designs of Providence that, in these times of trial for the Church, the ancient devotion to the august Virgin should live and

flourish amid the greatest part of the Christian world. May now the Christian nations, excited by Our exhortations, and inflamed by your appeals, seek the protection of Mary with an ardour growing greater day by day; let them cling more and more to the practice of the Rosary, to that devotion which our ancestors were in the habit of practicing, not only as an ever-ready remedy for their misfortunes, but as a whole badge of Christian piety. The heavenly Patroness of the human race will receive with joy these prayers and supplications, and will easily obtain that the good shall grow in virtue, and that the erring should return to salvation and repent; and that God who is the avenger of crime, moved to mercy and pity may deliver Christendom and civil society from all dangers, and restore to them peace so much desired.

11. Encouraged by this hope, We beseech God Himself, with the most earnest desire of Our heart, through her in whom he has placed the fulness of all good, to grant you. Venerable Brethren, every gift of heavenly blessing. As an augury and pledge of which, We lovingly impart to you, to your clergy, and to the people entrusted to your care, the Apostolic Benediction.

Given in Rome, at St. Peter's, the 1st of September, 1883, in the sixth year of Our Pontificate.

Superiore Anno

On the Recitation of the Rosary
Pope Leo XIII - August 30, 1884
To All Our Venerable Brethren the Patriarchs, Primates, Archbishops, and Bishops of the Catholic World in the Grace and Communion of the Apostolic See.

Venerable Brethren, Health and Apostolic Benediction.

Last year, as each of you is aware, We decreed by an Encyclical Letter that, to win the help of Heaven for the Church in her trials, the great Mother of God should be honored by the means of the most holy Rosary during the whole of the month of October. In this We followed both Our own impulse and the example of Our predecessors, who in times of difficulty were wont to have recourse with increased fervor to the Blessed Virgin, and to seek her aid with special prayers. That wish of Ours has been complied with, with such a willingness and unanimity that it is more than ever apparent how real is the religion and how great is the fervor of the Christian peoples, and how great is the trust everywhere placed in the heavenly patronage of the Virgin Mary. For Us, weighed down with the burden of such and so great trials and evils, We confess that the sight of such intensity of open piety and faith has been a great consolation, and even gives Us new courage for the facing, if that be the wish of God, of still greater trials. Indeed, from the spirit of prayer which is poured out over the house of David and the dwellers in Jerusalem, we have a confident hope that God will at length let Himself be touched and have pity upon the state of His Church, and give ear to the prayers coming to Him through her whom He has chosen to be the dispenser of all heavenly graces.

2. For these reasons, therefore, with the same causes in existence which impelled Us last year, as We have said, to rouse the piety of all, We have deemed it Our duty to exhort again this year the people of Christendom to persevere in that method and formula of prayer known as the Rosary of Mary, and thereby to merit the powerful patronage of the great Mother of God. In as much as the enemies of Christianity are so stubborn in their aims, its defenders must be equally staunch, especially as the heavenly help and the benefits which are bestowed on us by God are the more usually the fruits of our perseverance. It is good to recall to memory the example

of that illustrious widow, Judith — a type of the Blessed Virgin — who curbed the ill-judged impatience of the Jews when they attempted to fix, according to their own judgment, the day appointed by God for the deliverance of His city. The example should also be borne in mind of the Apostles, who awaited the supreme gift promised unto them of the Paraclete, and persevered unanimously in prayer with Mary the Mother of Jesus. For it is indeed, an arduous and exceeding weighty matter that is now in hand: it is to humiliate an old and most subtle enemy in the spread-out array of his power; to win back the freedom of the Church and of her Head; to preserve and secure the fortifications within which should rest in peace the safety and weal of human society. Care must be taken, therefore, that, in these times of mourning for the Church, the most holy devotion of the Rosary of Mary be assiduously and piously observed, the more so that this method of prayer being so arranged as to recall in turn all the mysteries of our salvation, is eminently fitted to foster the spirit of piety.

3. With respect to Italy, it is now most necessary to implore the intercession of the most powerful Virgin through the medium of the Rosary, since a misfortune, and not an imaginary one, is threatening — nay, rather is among us. The Asiatic cholera, having, under God's will, crossed the boundary within which nature seemed to have confined it, has spread through the crowded shores of a French port, and thence to the neighboring districts of Italian soil. — To Mary, therefore, we must fly — to her whom rightly and justly the Church entitles the dispenser of saving, aiding, and protecting gifts — that she, graciously hearkening to our prayers, may grant us the help they besought, and drive far from us the unclean plague.

4. We have therefore resolved that in this coming month of October, in which the sacred devotions to Our Virgin Lady of the Rosary are solemnized throughout the Catholic world, all the devotions shall again be observed which were commanded by Us this time last year. — We therefore decree and make order that from the 1st of October to the 2nd of November following in all the parish churches (curialibus templis), in all public churches dedicated to the Mother of God, or in such as are appointed by the Ordinary, five decades at least of the Rosary be recited, together with the Litany. If in the morning, the Holy Sacrifice will take place during these prayers; if in the evening, the Blessed Sacrament will be exposed for the adoration of the faithful; after which those present will receive the customary Benediction. We desire that, wherever it be lawful, the local

confraternity of the Rosary should make a solemn procession through the streets as a public manifestation of religious devotion.

5. That the heavenly treasures of the Church may be thrown open to all, We hereby renew every Indulgence granted by Us last year. To all those, therefore, who shall have assisted on the prescribed days at the public recital of the Rosary, and have prayed for Our intentions — to all those also who from legitimate causes shall have been compelled to do so in private — We grant for each occasion an Indulgence of seven years and seven times forty days. To those who, in the prescribed space of time shall have performed these devotions at least ten times — either publicly in the churches or from just causes in the privacy of their homes-and shall have expiated their sins by confession and have received Communion at the altar, We grant from the treasury of the Church a Plenary Indulgence. We also grant this full forgiveness of sins and plenary remission of punishment to all those who, either on the feast day itself of Our Blessed Lady of the Rosary, or on any day within the subsequent eight days, shall have washed the stains from their souls and have holily partaken of the Divine banquet, and shall have also prayed in any church to God and His most holy Mother for Our intentions. As We desire also to consult the interests of those who live in country districts, and are hindered, especially in the month of October, by their agricultural labors, We permit all We have above decreed, and also the holy Indulgences gainable in the month of October, to be postponed to the following months of November or December, according to the prudent decision of the Ordinaries.

6. We doubt not, Venerable Brethren, that rich and abundant fruits will be the result of these efforts, especially if God, by the bestowal of His heavenly graces, bring an added increase to the fields planted by Us and watered by your zeal. We are certain that the faithful of Christendom will hearken to the utterance of Our Apostolic authority with the same fervor of faith and piety of which they gave most ample evidence last year. May our Heavenly Patroness, invoked by us through the Rosary, graciously be with us and obtain that, all disagreements of opinion being removed and Christianity restored throughout the world, we may obtain from God the wished for peace in the Church. — In pledge of that boon, to you, your clergy, and the flock entrusted to your care, We lovingly bestow the Apostolic Benediction.

Given in Rome, at St. Peter's, the 30th of August, 1884, in the Seventh Year of Our Pontificate.

Quod Auctoritate

Proclaiming a Jubilee
Pope Leo XIII - December 22, 1885
To Our Venerable Brethren the Patriarchs, Primates, Archbishops, Bishops, and other Local Ordinaries, in the Grace and Communion of the Apostolic See.

Venerable Brethren, Health and Apostolic Benediction.

That which We, by the Apostolic authority, have more than once decreed, that an extraordinary year of Jubilee should be kept throughout the whole Christian world, and the treasures of heavenly gifts, the dispensation of which is in Our power, should be thrown open to the faithful — that with the favor of God We have determined to decree for the ensuing year. The advantages of this step will not escape you, Venerable Brethren, who are so familiar with the spirit of the age and the temper of the time, but there is a special reason now which makes Our decision seem more than usually opportune. In view of the fact that in Our recent Encyclical Letter We pointed out how important it is that the States should conform as closely as possible to truth and the Christian ideal, it will easily be understood how fitting it is that We should now use every effort to excite men, or to lead them back to the practice of Christian virtues. For a State is what the lives of the people make it: and just as the excellence of a ship or a house is dependent upon the good quality and the right adjustment of its component parts, so, unless the individual citizens lead good lives, the State cannot keep in the path of virtue, and without offending. Civil government and those things which constitute the public life of a country come into existence and perish by the act of men; and men almost always succeed in stamping the image of their opinions and their lives upon their public institutions. In order therefore that Our teaching may sink into men's minds, and what is the great thing, actually govern their daily lives, an attempt must be made to bring them to think and act like Christians, not less in public than in private.

2. And in this matter effort is the more needful because perils everywhere abound. The great virtues of our forefathers have in large measure disappeared; the most violent passions have claimed a freer indulgence; the madness of opinion which knows no restraint, or at least no effective restraint, every day extends further; of those whose principles are sound there are many who, through a misplaced timidity,

are frightened, and have not the courage even to speak out their opinions boldly, far less to translate them into deeds; everywhere the worst examples are affecting public morals; wicked societies which We ourselves have denounced before now, skilled in all evil arts, are doing their best to lead the people astray, and as far as they are able, to withdraw them from God, their duty, and Christianity.

3. Amid these many and pressing evils, which are the more serious because they are already of long duration, nothing must be left undone by Us which can afford any hope of relief. With this purpose, and in this hope, We proclaim a sacred Jubilee to all those who have their salvation at heart, and need to be reminded and exhorted to raise their thoughts, now busied with worldly matters, to the contemplation of heavenly things. And this with a gain not merely to the individuals themselves, but to the whole future well-being of the commonwealth, because in proportion as individual citizens advance along the path of perfection, there is a corresponding increase in the general rectitude and probity, in the public life and morals of the nation.

4. But you will observe, Venerable Brethren, that success will largely depend upon your industry and zeal, as it will be needful to prepare the people properly and carefully if they are to reap the fruits which are to be placed before them. We commit it to your judgment and prudence to place this matter in the hands of priests whom you may select, that by discourses fitted to the capacity of the crowd they may instruct them, and above all exhort them to that penance which, according to St. Augustine, consists in "the daily chastisement of the good and the faithful followers of Christ in which we strike our breasts, saying 'forgive us our sins.'" [1] With good reason We mention here in the first place that part of penance which consists of the voluntary punishment of the body. You know the temper of the times — how many there are who love to live delicately and shrink from whatever requires manhood and generosity; who, when ailments come, discover in them sufficient reasons for not obeying the salutary laws of the Church, thinking the burden laid upon them more than they can bear, when they are told to abstain from certain kinds of food or to fast during a few days in the year. It is not to be wondered at if, weakened by these habits of indulgence, they gradually give themselves up body and soul to the more imperious passions. It is therefore necessary to recall to the paths of moderation those who have fallen or who are likely to fall through this sort of effeminacy. Therefore those who speak to the people should lay it down persistently and clearly that

---

[1] Epistle 108

according not only to the law of the Gospel, but even to the dictates of natural reason, a man is bound to govern himself and keep his passions under strict control, and moreover, that sin cannot be expiated except by penance. That the virtue of which We have spoken may be durable, it will be prudent to put it in some sort under the safeguard and protection of a stable institution; you know well, venerable brothers, to what We allude; We mean that you should continue each one in his own diocese to protect and propagate the Third Order, called the Secular Order, of the Franciscan Friars. To keep up the spirit of penance in the Christian multitude nothing is more effectual than the example and the grace of the Patriarch Francis of Assisi, who combined with the greatest innocence of life so much zeal for mortification that the image of Jesus Christ crucified was not less visible in his life and conduct than in the signs which were supernaturally impressed upon him. The laws of his Order, which We have modified for the times, are as light to bear as they are effectual for the practice of Christian virtue.

5. In the second place, as every hope of safety lies in the protection and succor of our Heavenly Father in the midst of so great private and public necessities, We would earnestly desire to see confidence united with the revival of an assiduous zeal in prayer. In every great crisis of Christendom, and every time the Church was afflicted by evils within or dangers without, our forefathers, with their eyes lifted to Heaven in supplication, taught us how and when we should seek for the light of our souls, for the strength of virtue, and for help suited to the need. For deeply engraved upon men's minds were these precepts of Jesus Christ: "Ask and it shall be given you;" [2] "We ought always to pray and not to faint." [3] And with this teaching the word of the Apostle corresponds: "Pray without ceasing;" [4] "I desire, therefore, first of all that supplications, prayers, intercessions, and thanksgivings be made for all men." [5] Upon which subject St. John Chrysostom has left us this saying, not less true than ingenious, in the form of a comparison: "Even as man, who comes into the light of day naked and wanting all things, has been endowed by nature with hands to procure for himself all the necessaries of life; so in supernatural things, seeing that of himself he can do nothing, he has received from

---

[2] Matthew 7:7
[3] Luke 18:1
[4] I Thessalonians 5:17
[5] I Timothy 2:1

God the faculty of prayer, that he may use it wisely for the obtaining of all that is needful to his salvation."

6. From all this, Venerable Brethren, each one of you may gather how agreeable to Us and how commendable is the zeal with which at Our suggestion you have spread the devotion to the Most Holy Rosary, especially in these last years. Nor can We pass over the popular piety which has almost everywhere been excited by this method of prayer. Now you must watch with the greatest care that this devotion be practiced with even greater and greater fervor, and that it be persevered in without failing. And if We insist upon this exhortation, as We have already done several times, not one of you will be surprised, for you understand how important it is that this habit of the Rosary of Mary should flourish among Christians. And you are perfectly aware that this is a part and a beautiful form of that spirit of prayer of which we speak, and that it is at once admirably suited to our times, easy to practice, and fruitful in results. But as the first and the chief fruit of the Jubilee must be, as We have already pointed out, amendment of life and progress in virtue, We deem especially necessary the avoidance of that evil which We have not neglected to point out in Our past Encyclicals. We allude to those internal, and, as it were, domestic dissensions among some of ourselves; dissensions of which it is hardly possible to say how much they break or relax the bonds of charity, to the great detriment of souls. If We recall this to you once more, Venerable Brethren, who are the guardians of ecclesiastical discipline and of mutual charity, it is that We desire to see your watchfulness and your authority always directed to the prevention of so great an evil. By your warnings, your exhortations, your reproaches, urge all "to keep the unity of spirit in the bond of peace," induce the authors of the dissensions, if such there be, to return to their duty by the consideration which they should ever keep in mind that the only-begotten Son of God, even at the approach of His last torments, asked nothing more urgently of His Father than the mutual love of those who believed, or should believe, in Him, "that they may all be one, even as Thou, Father, art in Me, and I in Thee, that they also may be one in Us." [6]

7. Relying, therefore, on the mercy of the omnipotent God, and the authority of the Blessed Apostles St. Peter and St. Paul, and making use of that power of binding and loosing which our Lord has given to Us, though unworthy of it, We grant under the form of a General Jubilee a plenary indulgence to all the faithful of both sexes

---

[6] John 17:21

upon this condition and subject to this obligation, that during the coming year of 1886 they perform the things mentioned below.

8. The citizens and inhabitants of Rome must pay two visits to the Lateran, the Vatican, and the Liberian Basilicas, and pray there for some time to God according to Our intentions for the well-being and the exaltation of the Church, for the rooting out of all heresy, and for the conversion of all who are in error, and in accordance with Our intentions pour out prayers to God that concord may reign among Christian princes, and that peace and unity may be the lot of all the faithful. They must also fast for two days, only using the food usually allowed in times of penance, in addition to the forty days of Lent and other days set aside by the Church as fast days. They must also, after having properly confessed their sins, receive Holy Communion, and, in accordance with the advice of their confessor, give an alms, each according to his means, to the furthering of some work likely to promote the propagation and increase of the Catholic Church. Each may choose the object he prefers; but We think it well especially to name two, towards which assistance may be given with the greatest advantage; and of these each is an object which in many places is in need of help and aid, and fruitful in advantage, not less for the State than for the Church, We mean the Primary schools for boys and the Seminaries for the Clergy.

9. Those who reside outside Rome, in whatever part of the world they may live, must pay two visits at prescribed intervals to three churches to be appointed by you, Venerable Brethren, your Vicars or Officials, on your or their command, by those who have the charge of souls; or three visits if there are only two churches, or six visits if there is only one; and also must comply with all the conditions already laid down above. This indulgence may be applied by way of suffrage to the souls who have departed this life joined in charity with God. We give you power to reduce the number of the visits according to your judgment to certain churches in the case of chapters, congregations, as well secular as regular, communities, confraternities, universities, and colleges where the visits are made in procession.

10. Sailors and travelers may obtain the indulgence upon their return home, or their arrival at some fixed station, by visiting six times the principal church, or the parish church of the district, and complying with the other conditions which We have already laid down. In the case of regulars of either sex, and even in the case of persons belonging to enclosed orders, and also in the case of all others, whether ecclesiastical or lay, who are prevented either because they

are in prison, or through infirmity, or any other good reason, from fulfilling the above conditions, or some of them, the confessor has power to conmute for other pious works, and also has power to dispense from Communion children who have not yet made their First Communion. Moreover, We grant to all and each of the faithful, both lay and ecclesiastic, secular and regular, of whatever order and institute, and even of those which ought to be specially named, that they should choose for the purpose of the Jubilee any approved confessor they like; nuns, novices, and other women living in the cloister may avail themselves of this power provided the confessor chosen is approved for nuns. To confessors upon this occasion, and while the time of this Jubilee lasts, We grant all the faculties which were granted by Our Letters Apostolic of February 15th, 1879, beginning with the words Pontifices maximi; always excepting the things which were excepted in those Letters.

11. Finally let all do their best to gain the graces of heaven during this time by a special devotion to the great Mother of God. For We wish this Jubilee to be placed under the patronage of the Most Holy Rosary of the Virgin; and with her assistance We are confident that there will be many whose souls, set free by the cleansing away of the stains of sin, will be renewed by faith and piety and justice, not only to the hope of eternal salvation, but also as an earnest of a more peaceful time.

12. As a pledge of heavenly graces and a witness to Our fatherly goodwill towards you, We give from the bottom of Our heart the Apostolic Benediction to you and your Clergy, and the whole people committed to your care and watchfulness.

Given in Rome, at St. Peter's, on the twenty-second day of December, in the year 1885, the eighth of Our Pontificate.

Vi E Ben Noto

On the Rosary and Public Life
Pope Leo XIII - September 20, 1887
To the Bishops of Italy.

Venerable Brethren,

You know how We place amid present dangers Our confidence in the Glorious Virgin of the Holy Rosary, for the safety and prosperity of Christendom and the peace and tranquillity of the Church. Mindful that in moments of great trial, pastors and people have ever had recourse with entire confidence to the august Mother of God, in whose hands are all graces, certain too, that devotion to Our Lady of the Rosary is most opportune for the needs of these times, We have desired to revive everywhere this devotion, and to spread it far and wide among the faithful of the world. Oftentimes already We, in recommending the pious practice of devoting October to honoring Our Lady, have pointed out Our reasons and hope for so doing, and the forms to be observed; and the entire Church, docile to Our desires, has ever replied by special manifestations of devotion; and now is making ready to pay to Mary, during a whole month, a daily tribute of the devotion so dear to it. In such pious rivalry Italy has not been behind-hand, for devotion to Our Lady is deeply and widely rooted in this land; and We doubt not that this year too, Italy will set a glorious example of love for the august Mother of God, and will give Us fresh reasons for consolation and hope. Nevertheless We cannot do less than address to you, Venerable Brethren, a few words of exhortation, so that with particular and renewed zeal the month dedicated to the Most Holy Virgin of the Rosary may be sanctified in every diocese of Italy.

2. It is easy to imagine what reasons We have for doing this. Since God called Us to govern His Church on earth, We have sought to use every possible means that We deemed suitable, for the sanctification of souls and the extension of the reign of Jesus Christ. We have excepted from Our daily solicitude no nation and no people, mindful that Our Redeemer shed His precious blood on the Cross and opened the reign of grace and of glory for all. None, however, can be surprised that We showed special care for the Italian people, for Our Divine Master Jesus Christ chose, from out all the world, Italy to be the seat of His Vicar on earth, and in His providential designs appointed Rome to be the capital of the Catholic world. On this

account the Italian people is called upon to live close to the Father of the whole Christian family, and to share in a special way in his sorrows and his glory. Unfortunately We find in Italy much to sadden Our souls. Faith and Christian morals, the precious inheritance bequeathed by Our ancestors, and in all past times the glory of Our country and of Italy's great ones, are being attacked artfully and in covert ways, or even openly, with cynicism that is revolting, by a handful of men who seek to rob others of that faith and morality they have themselves lost. In this more especially is seen the work of the sects, and of those who are more or less their willing tools. Above all, in this city of Rome, where Christ's Vicar has his See are their efforts concentrated and their diabolical designs displayed with ferocious obstinacy.

3. We need not tell you, Venerable Brethren, with what bitterness Our soul is filled at seeing the danger there is for the salvation of so many of Our beloved children. And Our sorrow is greater because We find it impossible to oppose such great evil with that salutary efficacy We would desire and that We have the right to use, for you know, Venerable Brethren, and all the world knows, the state to which we are reduced. On this account We feel a still greater desire to call upon the Mother of God and to ask her help. Let all good Italians pray for their misguided brethren, for their common Father the Roman Pontiff, that God, in His infinite mercy, may hear and answer the prayers of a father and his sons. And Our most lively and sure hope is placed in the Queen of the Rosary, who has shown herself, since she has been invoked by that title, so ready to help the Church and Christian peoples in their necessities. Already have We recorded these glories and the great triumphs won over the Albigenses and other powerful enemies, glories and triumphs which have not only profited the Church, afflicted and persecuted, but also the temporal welfare of peoples and nations. Why in this hour of need should We not behold again such marvels of the power and goodness of the august Virgin, for the good of the Church and its Head, and of the whole Christian world, if the faithful only revive, on their part, the magnificent examples of piety given by their forefathers, under similar circumstances? And to make this most powerful Queen more and more propitious, We would honor her more and more in the invocation of the Rosary, and increase this devotion. And to this end We have made a double of the second class for all the Church of the Feast of the Rosary. And for the same purpose We ardently desire the Catholics of Italy, with lively faith, especially during this month of October, to

invoke this august Virgin and to do loving violence to her mother's heart, and to pray to her for the triumph of the Church and the Apostolic See, for the liberty of the Vicar of Jesus Christ on earth, and for peace and public prosperity. And, since the effects of such prayers will be proportionate to the dispositions of those offering them, We ardently exhort you, venerable brethren, devote all your care and zeal to kindle among those committed to your charge a strong, living and active faith, and to call on all to return by penance to grace and to the faithful fulfillment of; all their duties. Among such duties, considering the state of the times, must be reckoned as paramount an open and sincere profession of the faith and teaching of Jesus Christ, casting aside all human respect, and considering before all thing the interest of religion and the salvation of souls. It cannot be concealed that, although thanks to the mercy of God religious feeling is strong and widely spread among Italians, nevertheless by the evil influence of men and the times religious indifference is on the increase, and hence there is lessening of that respect and filial love for the Church which was the glory of our ancestors and in which they placed their highest ambition. Let it be your work, venerable brethren, to revive this Christian feeling among your people, an interest in the Catholic cause, a confidence in Our Lady's help, and a spirit of prayer. It is certain that the august Queen, invoked thus well by her man sons, would deign to hear their prayer, console Us in Our sorrow, and crown Our efforts for the Church and for Italy, by granting better times to both. With these desires, We bestow on you venerable brethren, and the clergy and people committed to your care, the Apostolic Benediction as a promise of graces and favors of the highest kind from heaven.

Given at the Vatican this 20th day of September 1887.

Octobri Mense 1891

On the Rosary
Pope Leo XIII - September 22, 1891
To Our Venerable Brethren the Patriarchs, Primates, Archbishops, Bishops, and other Ordinaries having Grace and Communion with the Apostolic See.

Venerable Brethren, Greeting and Apostolic Benediction.

At the coming of the month of October, dedicated and consecrated as it is to the Blessed Virgin of the Rosary, we recall with satisfaction the instant exhortations which in preceding years We addressed to you, venerable brethren, desiring, as We did, that the faithful, urged by your authority and by your zeal, should redouble their piety towards the august Mother of God, the mighty helper of Christians, and should pray to her throughout the month, invoking her by that most holy rite of the Rosary which the Church, especially in the passage of difficult times, has ever used for the accomplishment of all desires. This year once again do We publish Our wishes, once again do We encourage you by the same exhortations. We are persuaded to this in love for the Church, whose sufferings, far from mitigating, increase daily in number and in gravity. Universal and well-known are the evils we deplore: war made upon the sacred dogmas which the Church holds and transmits; derision cast upon the integrity of that Christian morality which she has in keeping; enmity declared, with the impudence of audacity and with criminal malice, against the very Christ, as though the Divine work of Redemption itself were to be destroyed from its foundation — that work which, indeed, no adverse power shall ever utterly abolish or destroy.

2. No new events are these in the career of the Church militant. Jesus foretold them to His disciples. That she may teach men the truth and may guide them to eternal salvation, she must enter upon a daily war; and throughout the course of ages she has fought, even to martyrdom, rejoicing and glorifying herself in nothing more than in the occasion of signing her cause with her Founder's blood, the sure and certain pledge of the victory whereof she holds the promise. Nevertheless we must not conceal the profound sadness with which this necessity of constant war afflicts the righteous. It is indeed a cause of great sorrow that so many should be deterred and led astray by error and enmity to God; that so many should be indifferent to all forms of

religion, and should finally become estranged from faith; that so many Catholics should be such in name only, and should pay to religion no honor or worship. And still sadder and more beset with anxieties grows the soul at the thought of the fruitful source of most manifold evils existing in the organization of States that allow no place to the Church, and that oppose her championship of holy virtue. This is truly a terrible manifestation of the just vengeance of God, Who allows blindness of soul to darken upon the nations that forsake Him. These are evils that cry aloud, that cry of themselves with a daily increasing voice. It is absolutely necessary that the Catholic voice should also call to God with unwearied instance, "without ceasing;" [7] that the Faithful should pray not only in their own homes, but in public, gathered together under the sacred roof; that they should beseech urgently the all-foreseeing God to deliver the Church from evil men [8] and to bring back the troubled nations to good sense and reason, by the light and love of Christ.

    3. Wonderful and beyond hope or belief is this. The world goes on its laborious way, proud of its riches, of its power, of its arms, of its genius; the Church goes onward along the course of ages with an even step, trusting in God only, to Whom, day and night, she lifts her eyes and her suppliant hands. Even though in her prudence she neglects not the human aid which Providence and the times afford her, not in these does she put her trust, which rests in prayer, in supplication, in the invocation of God. Thus it is that she renews her vital breath; the diligence of her prayer has caused her, in her aloofness from worldly things and in her continual union with the Divine will, to live the tranquil and peaceful life of Our very Lord Jesus Christ; being herself the image of Christ, Whose happy and perpetual joy was hardly marred by the horror of the torments He endured for us. This important doctrine of Christian wisdom has been ever believed and practiced by Christians worthy of the name. Their prayers rise to God eagerly and more frequently when the cunning and the violence of the perverse afflict the Church and her supreme Pastor. Of this the faithful of the Church in the East gave an example that should be offered to the imitation of posterity. Peter, Vicar of Jesus Christ, and first Pontiff of the Church, had been cast into prison, loaded with chains by the guilty Herod, and left for certain death. None could carry him help or snatch him from the peril. But there was the certain help that fervent prayer wins from God. The Church, as the sacred story tells us, made prayer

---

[7]   I Thessalonians 5:17
[8]   II Thessalonians 3:2

without ceasing to God for him; [9] and the greater was the fear of a misfortune, the greater was the fervor of all who prayed to God. After the granting of their desires the miracle stood revealed; and Christians still celebrate with a joyous gratitude the marvel of the deliverance of Peter. Christ has given us a still more memorable instance, a Divine instance, so that the Church might be formed not upon his precepts only, but upon His example also. During His whole life He had given Himself to frequent and fervent prayer, and in the supreme hours in the Garden of Gethsemane, when His soul was filled with bitterness and sorrow unto death, He prayed to His Father and prayed repeatedly. [10] It was not for Himself that He prayed thus, for He feared nothing and needed nothing, being God; He prayed for us, for His Church, whose prayers and future tears He already then accepted with joy, to give them back in mercies.

    4. But since the salvation of our race was accomplished by the mystery of the Cross, and since the Church, dispenser of that salvation after the triumph of Christ, was founded upon earth and instituted, Providence established a new order for a new people. The consideration of the Divine counsels is united to the great sentiment of religion. The Eternal Son of God, about to take upon Him our nature for the saving and ennobling of man, and about to consummate thus a mystical union between Himself and all mankind, did not accomplish His design without adding there the free consent of the elect Mother, who represented in some sort all human kind, according to the illustrious and just opinion of St. Thomas, who says that the Annunciation was effected with the consent of the Virgin standing in the place of humanity. [11] With equal truth may it be also affirmed that, by the will of God, Mary is the intermediary through whom is distributed unto us this immense treasure of mercies gathered by God, for mercy and truth were created by Jesus Christ. [12] Thus as no man goeth to the Father but by the Son, so no man goeth to Christ but by His Mother. How great are the goodness and mercy revealed in this design of God! What a correspondence with the frailty of man! We believe in the infinite goodness of the Most High, and we rejoice in it; we believe also in His justice and we fear it. We adore the beloved Savior, lavish of His blood and of His life; we dread the inexorable Judge. Thus do those whose actions have disturbed their consciences

---

[9] Acts 12:5
[10] Luke 22:44
[11] Summa Part III Question 30 Article 1
[12] John 1:17

need an intercessor mighty in favor with God, merciful enough not to reject the cause of the desperate, merciful enough to lift up again towards hope in the divine mercy the afflicted and the broken down. Mary is this glorious intermediary; she is the mighty Mother of the Almighty; but-what is still sweeter — she is gentle, extreme in tenderness, of a limitless loving-kindness. As such God gave her to us. Having chosen her for the Mother of His only begotten Son, He taught her all a mother's feeling that breathes nothing but pardon and love. Such Christ desired she should be, for He consented to be subject to Mary and to obey her as a son a mother. Such He proclaimed her from the cross when he entrusted to her care and love the whole of the race of man in the person of His disciple John. Such, finally, she proves herself by her courage in gathering in the heritage of the enormous labors of her Son, and in accepting the charge of her maternal duties towards us all.

5. The design of this most dear mercy, realized by God in Mary and confirmed by the testament of Christ, was comprehended at the beginning, and accepted with the utmost joy by the Holy Apostles and the earliest believers. It was the counsel and teaching of the venerable Fathers of the Church. All the nations of the Christian age received it with one mind; and even when literature and tradition are silent there is a voice that breaks from every Christian breast and speaks with all eloquence. No other reason is needed that that of a Divine faith which, by a powerful and most pleasant impulse, persuades us towards Mary. Nothing is more natural, nothing more desirable than to seek a refuge in the protection and in the loyalty of her to whom we may confess our designs and our actions, our innocence and our repentance, our torments and our joys, our prayers and our desires — all our affairs. All men, moreover, are filled with the hope and confidence that petitions which might be received with less favor from the lips of unworthy men, God will accept when they are recommended by the most Holy Mother, and will grant with all favors. The truth and the sweetness of these thoughts bring to the soul an unspeakable comfort; but they inspire all the more compassion for those who, being without Divine faith, honor not Mary and have her not for their mother; for those also who, holding Christian faith, dare to accuse of excess the devotion to Mary, thereby sorely wounding filial piety.

6. This storm of evils, in the midst of which the Church struggles so strenuously, reveals to all her pious children the holy duty whereto they are bound to pray to God with instance, and the manner

in which they may give to their prayers the greater power. Faithful to the religious example of our fathers, let us have recourse to Mary, our holy Sovereign. Let us entreat, let us beseech, with one heart, Mary, the Mother of Jesus Christ, our Mother. "Show thyself to be a mother; cause our prayers to be accepted by Him Who, born for us, consented to be thy Son." [13]

7. Now, among the several rites and manners of paying honor to the Blessed Mary, some are to be preferred, inasmuch as we know them to be most powerful and most pleasing to our Mother; and for this reason we specially mention by name and recommend the Rosary. The common language has given the name of corona to this manner of prayer, which recalls to our minds the great mysteries of Jesus and Mary united in joys, sorrows, and triumphs. The contemplation of these august mysteries, contemplated in their order, affords to faithful souls a wonderful confirmation of faith, protection against the disease of error, and increase of the strength of the soul. The soul and memory of him who thus prays, enlightened by faith, are drawn towards these mysteries by the sweetest devotion, are absorbed therein and are surprised before the work of the Redemption of mankind, achieved at such a price and by events so great. The soul is filled with gratitude and love before these proofs of Divine love; its hope becomes enlarged and its desire is increased for those things which Christ has prepared for such as have united themselves to Him in imitation of His example and in participation in His sufferings. The prayer is composed of words proceeding from God Himself, from the Archangel Gabriel, and from the Church; full of praise and of high desires; and it is renewed and continued in an order at once fixed and various; its fruits are ever new and sweet.

8. Moreover, we may well believe that the Queen of Heaven herself has granted an especial efficacy to this mode of supplication, for it was by her command and counsel that the devotion was begun and spread abroad by the holy Patriarch Dominic as a most potent weapon against the enemies of the faith at an epoch not, indeed, unlike our own, of great danger to our holy religion. The heresy of the Albigenses had in effect, one while covertly, another while openly, overrun many countries, and this most vile offspring of the Manicheans, whose deadly errors it reproduced, were the cause in stirring up against the Church the most bitter animosity and a virulent persecution. There seemed to be no human hope of opposing this fanatical and most pernicious sect when timely succor came from on

---

[13] From the Sacred Liturgy

high through the instrument of Mary's Rosary. Thus under the favor of the powerful Virgin, the glorious vanquisher of all heresies, the forces of the wicked were destroyed and dispersed, and faith issued forth unharmed and more shining than before. All manner of similar instances are widely recorded, and both ancient and modern history furnish remarkable proofs of nations saved from perils and winning benedictions therefrom. There is another signal argument in favor of this devotion, inasmuch as from the very moment of its institution it was immediately encouraged and put into most frequent practice by all classes of society. In truth, the piety of the Christian people honors, by many titles and in multiform ways, the Divine Mother, who, alone most admirable among all creatures, shines resplendent in unspeakable glory. But this title of the Rosary, this mode of prayer which seems to contain, as it were, a final pledge of affection, and to sum up in itself the honor due to Our Lady, has always been highly cherished and widely used in private and in public, in homes and in families, in the meetings of confraternities, at the dedication of shrines, and in solemn processions; for there has seemed to be no better means of conducting sacred solemnities, or of obtaining protection and favors.

9. Nor may we permit to pass unnoticed the especial Providence of God displayed in this devotion; for through the lapse of time religious fervor has sometimes seemed to diminish in certain nations, and even this pious method of prayer has fallen into disuse; but piety and devotion have again flourished and become vigorous in a most marvelous manner, when, either through the grave situation of the commonwealth or through some pressing public necessity, general recourse has been had — more to this than to even other means of obtaining help — to the Rosary, whereby it has been restored to its place of honor on the altars. But there is no need to seek for examples of this power in a past age, since we have in the present a signal instance of it. In these times — so troublous (as we have said before) for the Church, and so heartrending for ourselves — set as We are by the Divine will at the helm, it is still given Us to note with admiration the great zeal and fervor with which Mary's Rosary is honored and recited in every place and nation of the Catholic world. And this circumstance, which assuredly is to be attributed to the Divine action and direction upon men, rather than to the wisdom and efforts of individuals, strengthens and consoles Our heart, filling Us with great hope for the ultimate and most glorious triumph of the Church under the auspices of Mary.

10. But there are some who, whilst they honestly agree with what We have said, yet because their hopes — especially as regard the peace and tranquillity of the Church — have not yet been fulfilled, nay, rather because troubles seem to augment, have ceased to pray with diligence and fervor, in a fit of discouragement. Let these look into themselves and labor that the prayers they address to God may be made in a proper spirit, according to the precept of our Lord Jesus Christ. And if there be such, let them reflect how unworthy and how wrong it is to wish to assign to Almighty God the time and the manner of giving His assistance, since He owes nothing to us, and when He hearkens to our supplications and crowns our merits, He only crowns His own innumerable benefits; [14] and when He complies least with our wishes it is as a good father towards his children, having pity on their childishness and consulting their advantage. But as regards the prayers which we join to the suffrages of the heavenly citizens, and offer humbly to God to obtain His mercy for the Church, they are always favorably received and heard, and either obtain for the Church great and imperishable benefits, or their influence is temporarily withheld for a time of greater need. In truth, to these supplications is added an immense weight and grace — the prayers and merits of Christ Our Lord, Who has loved the Church and has delivered Himself up for her to sanctify her . . . so that He should be glorified in her. [15] He is her Sovereign Head, holy, innocent, always living to make intercession for us, on whose prayers and supplication we can always by divine authority rely. As for what concerns the exterior and temporal prosperity of the Church, it is evident that she has to cope with most malicious and powerful adversaries. Too often has she suffered at their hands the abolition of her rights, the diminution and oppression of her liberties, scorn and affronts to her authority, and every conceivable outrage. And if in their wickedness her enemies have not accomplished all the injury they had resolved upon and striven to do, they nevertheless seem to go on unchecked. But, despite them the Church, amidst all these conflicts, will always stand out and increase in greatness and glory. Nor can human reason rightly understand why evil, apparently so dominant, should yet be so restricted as regards its results; whilst the Church, driven into straits, comes forth glorious and triumphant. And she ever remains more steadfast in virtue because she draws men to the acquisition of the ultimate good. And since this is her mission, her prayers must have much power to effect the end and

---

[14] Saint Augustine Epistle 194
[15] Ephesians 5:25-27

purpose of God's providential and merciful designs towards men. Thus, when men pray with and through the Church, they at length obtain what Almighty God has designed from all eternity to bestow upon mankind. [16] The subtlety of the human intelligence fails now to grasp the high designs of Providence; but the time will come when, through the goodness of God, causes and effects will be made clear, and the marvelous power and utility of prayer will be shown forth. Then it will be seen how many in the midst of a corrupt age have kept themselves pure and inviolate from all concupiscence of the flesh and the spirit, working out their sanctification in the fear of God; [17] how others, when exposed to the danger of temptation, have without delay restrained themselves gaining new strength for virtue from the peril itself; how others, having fallen, have been seized with the ardent desire to be restored to the embraces of a compassionate God. Therefore, with these reflections before them, We beseech all again and again not to yield to the deceits of the old enemy, nor for any cause whatsoever to cease from the duty of prayer. Let their prayers be persevering, let them pray without intermission; let their first care be to supplicate for the sovereign good-the eternal salvation of the whole world, and the safety of the Church. Then they may ask from God other benefits for the use and comfort of life, returning thanks always, whether their desires are granted or refused, as to a most indulgent father. Finally, may they converse with God with the greatest piety and devotion according to the example of the Saints, and that of our Most Holy Master and Redeemer, with great cries and tears. [18]

    11. Our fatherly solicitude urges Us to implore of God, the Giver of all good gifts, not merely the spirit of prayer, but also that of holy penance for all the sons of the Church. And whilst We make this most earnest supplication, We exhort all and each one to the practice with equal fervor of both these virtues combined. Thus prayer fortifies the soul, makes it strong for noble endeavors, leads it up to divine things: penance enables us to overcome ourselves, especially our bodies — most inveterate enemies of reason and the evangelical law. And it is very clear that these virtues unite well with each other, assist each other mutually, and have the same object, namely, to detach man born for heaven from perishable objects, and to raise him up to heavenly commerce with God. On the other hand, the mind that is excited by passions and enervated by pleasure is insensible to the

---

[16] Summa Part II-II Question 83 Article 2
[17] II Corinthians 7:1
[18] Hebrews 5:7

delights of heavenly things, and makes cold and neglectful prayers quite unworthy of being accepted by God. We have before Our eyes examples of the penance of holy men whose prayers and supplications were consequently most pleasing to God, and even obtained miracles. They governed and kept assiduously in subjection their minds and hearts and wills. They accepted with the greatest joy and humility the doctrines of Christ and the teachings of His Church. Their unique desire was to advance in the science of God; nor had their actions any other object than the increase of His glory. They restrained most severely their passions, treated their bodies rudely and harshly, abstaining from even permitted pleasures through love of virtue. And therefore most deservedly could they have said with the Apostle Paul, our conversation is in Heaven: [19] hence the potent efficacy of their prayers in appeasing and in supplicating the Divine Majesty. It is clear that not every one is obliged or able to attain to these heights; nevertheless, each one should correct his life and morals in his own measure in satisfaction to the Divine justice: for it is to those who have endured voluntary sufferings in this life that the reward of virtue is vouchsafed. Moreover, when in the mystical body of Christ, which is the Church, all the members are united and flourish, it results, according to St. Paul, that the joy or pain of one member is shared by all the rest, so that if one of the brethren in Christ is suffering in mind or body the others come to his help and succor him as far as in them lies. The members are solicitous in regard of each other, and if one member suffer all the members suffer in sympathy, and if one member rejoice all the others rejoice also. But you are the body of Christ, members of one body. [20] But in this illustration of charity, following the example of Christ, Who in the immensity of His love gave up His life to redeem us from sin, paying Himself the penalties incurred by others, in this is the great bond of perfection by which the faithful are closely united with the heavenly citizens and with God. Above all, acts of holy penance are so numerous and varied and extend over such a wide range, that each one may exercise them frequently with a cheerful and ready will without serious or painful effort.

12. And now, venerable brethren, your remarkable and exalted piety towards the Most Holy Mother of God, and your charity and solicitude for the Christian flock, are full of abundant promise: Our heart is full of desire for those wondrous fruits which, on many occasions, the devotion of Catholic people to Mary has brought forth;

---

[19] Philippians 3:20
[20] I Corinthians 12:25-27

already We enjoy them deeply and abundantly in anticipation. At your exhortation and under your direction, therefore, the faithful, especially during this ensuing month, will assemble around the solemn altars of this august Queen and most benign Mother, and weave and offer to her, like devoted children, the mystic garland so pleasing to her of the Rosary. All the privileges and indulgences We have herein before conceded are confirmed and ratified. [21]

13. How grateful and magnificent a spectacle to see in the cities, and towns, and villages, on land and sea — wherever the Catholic faith has penetrated — many hundreds of thousands of pious people uniting their praises and prayers with one voice and heart at every moment of the day, saluting Mary, invoking Mary, hoping everything through Mary. Through her may all the faithful strive to obtain from her Divine Son that the nations plunged in error may return to the Christian teaching and precepts, in which is the foundation of the public safety and the source of peace and true happiness. Through her may they steadfastly endeavor for that most desirable of all blessings, the restoration of the liberty of our Mother, the Church, and the tranquil possession of her rights — rights which have no other object than the careful direction of men's dearest interests, from the exercise of which individuals and nations have never suffered injury, but have derived, in all time, numerous and most precious benefits.

14. And for you, venerable brethren, through the intercession of the Queen of the Most Holy Rosary, We pray Almighty God to grant you heavenly gifts, and greater and more abundant strength, and aid to accomplish the charge of your pastoral office. As a pledge of which We most lovingly bestow upon you and upon the clergy and people committed to your care, the Apostolic Benediction.

Given at Rome, St. Peter's, the 22nd day of September, 1891, in the fourteenth year of Our Pontificate.

---

[21] Cf. ep. encycl. "Supremi Apostolatus officio" (September 1, 1893); ep. encycl. "Supreriore anno" (August 30, 1884); decree S. R. C. "Inter plurimos" (August 20, 1885); ep. encycl. "Quamquam pluries" (August 15, 1889).

Magnae Dei Matris

On the Rosary
Pope Leo XIII - September 8, 1892
To Our Venerable Brethren, the Patriarchs, Primates, Archbishops, and other Ordinaries in Peace and Communion with the Apostolic See.

As often as the occasion arises to stimulate and intensify the love and veneration of the Christian people for Mary, the great Mother of God, We are filled with wondrous satisfaction and joy, as by a subject which is not only of prime importance in itself and profitable in countless ways, but which also perfectly accords with the inmost sentiments of Our heart. For the holy reverence for Mary which We experienced from Our tenderest years, has grown greater and has taken firmer hold of Our soul with Our advancing age.

2. As time went on, it became more and more evident how deserving of love and honor was she whom God Himself was the first to love, and loved so much more than any other that, after elevating her high above all the rest of His creation and adorning her with His richest gifts, He made her His Mother. The many and splendid proofs of her bounty and beneficence toward us, which We remember with deep gratitude and which move Us to tears, still further encourage and strongly inflame Our filial reverence for her. Throughout the many dreadful events of every kind which the times have brought to pass, always with her have We sought refuge, always to her have We lifted up pleading and confident eyes. And in all the hopes and fears, the joys and sorrows, that We confided to her, the thought was constantly before Us to ask her to assist Us at all times as Our gracious Mother and to obtain this greatest of favors: that We might be able, in return, to show her the heart of a most devoted son.

3. When, then, it came to pass in the secret design of God's providence that We were chosen to fill this Chair of St. Peter and to take the place of the Person of Christ Himself in the Church, worried by the enormous burden of the office and finding no ground for reliance upon Our own strength, We hastened with fervent zeal to implore the divine aid through the maternal intercession of the ever blessed Virgin. Never has Our hope, We are happy to acknowledge, at any time of Our life but more especially since We began to exercise the Supreme Apostolate, failed in the course of events to bear fruit or bring Us comfort. Thus encouraged, Our hope today mounts more

confidently than ever to beseech many more and even greater blessings through her favor and mediation, which will profit alike the salvation of Christ's flock and the happy increase of His Church's glory.

4. It is, therefore, a fitting and opportune time, Venerable Brethren, for Us to induce all Our children — exhorting them through you — to plan on celebrating the coming month of October, consecrated to our Lady as the august Queen of the Rosary, with the fervent and wholehearted devotion which the necessities weighing upon Us demand.

5. It is only too plain how many and of what nature are the corrupting agencies by which the wickedness of the world deceitfully strives to weaken and completely uproot from souls their Christian faith and the respect for God's law on which faith is fed and depends for its effectiveness. Already the fields cultivated by our Lord are everywhere turning into a wilderness abounding in ignorance of the Faith, in error and vice, as though blown upon by some hideous pest. And to add to the anguish of this thought, so far from putting a check on such insolent and destructive depravity, or imposing the punishment deserved, they who can and should correct matters seem in many cases, by their indifference or open connivance, to increase the spirit of evil.

6. We have good reason to deplore the public institutions in which the teaching of the sciences and arts is purposely so organized that the name of God is passed over in silence or visited with vituperation; to deplore the license — growing more shameless by the day — of the press in publishing whatever it pleases, and the license of speech in addressing any kind of insult to Christ our God and His Church. And We deplore no less the consequent laxity and apathy in the practice of the Catholic religion which if not quite open apostasy from the Faith, is certainly going to prove an easy road to it, since it is a manner of life having nothing in common with faith. Nobody who ponders this disorder and the surrender of the most fundamental principles will be astonished if afflicted nations everywhere are groaning under the heavy hand of God's vengeance and stand anxious and trembling in fear of worse calamities.

7. Now, to appease the might of an outraged God and to bring that health of soul so needed by those who are sorely afflicted, there is nothing better than devout and persevering prayer, provided it be joined with a love for and practice of Christian life. And both of these, the spirit of prayer and the practice of Christian life, are best attained through the devotion of the Rosary of Mary.

8. The well-known origin of the Rosary, illustrated in celebrated monuments of which we have made frequent mention, bears witness to its remarkable efficacy. For, in the days when the Albigensian sect, posing as the champion of pure faith and morals, but in reality introducing the worst kind of anarchy and corruption, brought many a nation to its utter ruin, the Church fought against it and the other infamous factions associated with it, not with troops and arms, but chiefly with the power of the most holy Rosary, the devotion which the Mother of God taught to our Father Dominic in order that he might propagate it. By this means the Church triumphed magnificently over every obstacle and provided for the salvation of her children not only in that trial but in others like it afterward, always with the same glorious success. For this reason, now, when human affairs have taken the course which We deplore, bringing affection to the Church and ruin to the State, all of us have the duty to unite our voice in prayer, with like devotion, to the holy Mother of God, beseeching her that we too may rejoice, as we ardently desire, in experiencing the same power of her Rosary.

9. When we have recourse to Mary in prayer, we are having recourse to the Mother of mercy, who is so well disposed toward us that, whatever the necessity that presses upon us especially in attaining eternal life, she is instantly at our side of her own accord, even though she has not been invoked. She dispenses grace with a generous hand from that treasure with which from the beginning she was divinely endowed in fullest abundance that she might be worthy to be the Mother of God. By the fullness of grace which confers on her the most illustrious of her many titles, the Blessed Virgin is infinitely superior to all the hierarchies of men and angels, the one creature who is closest of all to Christ. "It is a great thing in any saint to have grace sufficient for the salvation of many souls; but to have enough to suffice for the salvation of everybody in the world. is the greatest of all; and this is found in Christ and in the Blessed Virgin." [22]

10. It is impossible to say how pleasing and gratifying to her it is when we greet her with the Angelic Salutation, "full of grace"; and in repeating it, fashion these words of praise into ritual crowns for her. For every time we say them, we recall the memory of her exalted dignity and of the Redemption of the human race which God began through her. We likewise bring to mind the divine and everlasting bond which links her with the joys and sorrows, the humiliations and triumphs of Christ in directing and helping mankind to eternal life.

---

[22] Saint Thomas Aquinas on the Angelic Salutation (Hail Mary)

11. It pleased Christ to take upon Himself the Son of Man, and to become thereby our Brother, in order that His mercy to us might be shown most openly; for "it behooved him in all things to be made like unto his brethren that he might become a merciful and faithful high priest before God." [23] Likewise because Mary was chosen to be the Mother of Christ, our Lord and our Brother, the unique prerogative was given her above all other mothers to show her mercy to us and to pour it out upon us. Besides, as we are indebted to Christ for sharing in some way with us the right, which is peculiarly His own, of calling God our Father and possessing Him as such, we are in like manner indebted to Him for His loving generosity in sharing with us the right to call Mary our Mother and to cherish her as such.

12. While nature itself made the name of mother the sweetest of all names and has made motherhood the very model of tender and solicitous love, no tongue is eloquent enough to put in words what every devout soul feels, namely how intense is the flame of affectionate and active charity which glows in Mary, in her who is truly our mother not in a human way but through Christ. Nobody knows and comprehends so well as she everything that concerns us: what helps we need in life; what dangers, public or private, threaten our welfare; what difficulties and evils surround us; above all, how fierce is the fight we wage with ruthless enemies of our salvation. In these and in all other troubles of life her power is most far-reaching. Her desire to use it is most ardent to bring consolation, strength, and help of every kind to children who are dear to her.

13. Accordingly, let us approach Mary confidently, wholeheartedly beseeching her by the bonds of her motherhood which unite her so closely to Jesus and at the same time to us. Let us with deepest devotion invoke her constant aid in the prayer which she herself has indicated and which is most acceptable to her. Then with good reason shall we rest with an easy and joyous mind under the protection of the best of mothers.

14. To this commendation of the Rosary which follows from the very nature of the prayer, We may add that the Rosary offers an easy way to present the chief mysteries of the Christian religion and to impress them upon the mind; and this commendation is one of the most beautiful of all. For it is mainly by faith that a man sets out on the straight and sure path to God and learns to revere in mind and heart His supreme majesty, His sovereignty over the whole of creation, His unsounded power, wisdom, and providence. For he who comes to God

---

[23] Hebrews 2:17

must believe that God exists and is a rewarder to those who seek Him. Moreover, because God's eternal Son assumed our humanity and shone before us as the Way, the Truth, and the Life, our faith must include the lofty mysteries of the august Trinity of divine Persons and of the Father's only-begotten Son made Man: "This is eternal life: that they may know thee, the only true God, and Jesus Christ, whom thou hast sent." [24]

15. God gave us a most precious blessing when He gave us faith. By this gift we are not only raised above the level of human things, to contemplate and share in the divine nature, but are also furnished with the means of meriting the rewards of heaven; and therefore the hope is encouraged and strengthened that we shall one day look upon God, not in the shadowy images of His creatures, but in the fullest light, and shall enjoy Him forever as the Supreme Goodness. But the Christian is kept so busy by the various affairs of life and wanders so easily into matters of little importance, that unless he be helped with frequent reminders, the truths which are of first importance and necessity are little by little forgotten; and then faith begins to grow weak and may even perish.

16. To ward off these exceedingly great dangers of ignorance from her children, the Church, which never relaxes her vigilant and diligent care, has been in the habit of looking for the staunchest support of faith in the Rosary of Mary. And indeed in the Rosary, along with the most beautiful and efficacious prayer arranged in an orderly pattern, the chief mysteries of our religion follow one another, as they are brought before our mind for contemplation: first of all the mysteries in which the Word was made flesh and Mary, the inviolate Virgin and Mother, performed her maternal duties for Him with a holy joy; there come then the sorrows, the agony and death of the suffering Christ, the price at which the salvation of our race was accomplished; then follow the mysteries full of His glory; His triumph over death, the Ascension into heaven, the sending of the Holy Ghost, the resplendent brightness of Mary received among the stars, and finally the everlasting glory of all the saints in heaven united with the glory of the Mother and her Son.

17. This uninterrupted sequence of wonderful events the Rosary frequently and perseveringly recalls to the minds of the faithful and presents almost as though they were unfolding before our eyes: and this, flooding the souls of those who devoutly recite it with a sweetness of piety that never grows weary, impresses and stirs them as

---

[24] John 17:3

though they were listening to the very voice of the Blessed Mother explaining the mysteries and conversing with them at length about their salvation.

18. It will not, then, seem too much to say that in places, families, and nations in which the Rosary of Mary retains its ancient honor, the loss of faith through ignorance and vicious error need not be feared.

19. There is still another and not lesser advantage which the Church earnestly seeks for her children from the Rosary, and that is the faithful regulation of their lives and their conduct in keeping with the rules and precepts of their holy religion. For if, as we all know from Holy Scripture, "faith without works is dead." [25] — because faith draws its life from charity and charity flowers forth in a profusion of holy actions — then the Christian will gain nothing for eternal life from his faith unless his life be ordered in accordance with what faith prescribes. "What shall it profit, my brethren, if a man say he hath faith, but hath not works? Shall faith be able to save him?" [26] A man of this sort will incur a much heavier rebuke from Christ the Judge than those who are, unfortunately, ignorant of Christian faith and its teaching: they, unlike the former, who believes one thing and practices another, have some excuse or at least are less blameworthy, because they lack the light of the Gospel.

20. In order therefore that the faith we profess may the better bring forth a harvest of fruits in keeping with its nature, while the mind is dwelling on mysteries of the Rosary the heart is wonderfully enkindled by them to make virtuous resolutions. What an example we have set before us! This shines forth everywhere in our Lord's work of salvation. Almighty God, in the excess of His love for us, takes upon Himself the form of lowly man. He dwells in our midst as one of the multitude, converses with us as a friend, instructs and teaches the way of justice to individuals and to multitudes. In His discourse He is the teacher unexcelled; in the authority of His teaching He is God. To all He shows Himself a doer of good; He relieves the sick of the ills of their bodies and, with paternal compassion, heals the most serious sickness of their souls. Those above all whom sorrow troubles or whom the weight of worry crushes, He comforts with the gentle invitation: "Come to me, all you that labor, and are burdened, and I will refresh you." [27] Then into us, at rest in His embrace, He breathes

---

[25] James 2:20
[26] James 2:14
[27] Matthew 11:28

that mystic fire which He has brought to all men, and benignly imbues us with the meekness and humility of His own heart, with the hope that, by the practice of these virtues, we may share the true and solid peace of which He is the Author: "Learn of me, because I am meek, and humble of heart; and you shall find rest to your souls." [28] For Himself, in return for that light of heavenly wisdom and that stupendous abundance of blessings which only He could merit for mankind, He suffers the hatred of men and their most atrocious insults; and, nailed to the cross, He pours out His blood and yields up His soul, holding it to be the highest glory to beget life in men by His death.

21. It would be utterly impossible for anyone to meditate on and attentively consider these most precious memorials of our loving Redeemer and not have a heart on fire with gratitude to Him. Such is the power of a faith sincerely practiced that, through the light it brings to man's mind and the vigor with which it moves his heart, he will straightway set out in the footsteps of Christ and follow them through every obstacle, making his own a protestation worthy of a St. Paul: "Who then shall separate us from the love of Christ? Shall tribulation? or distress? or famine? or nakedness? or danger? or persecution? or the sword?" [29] "I live, now not I; but Christ liveth in me." [30]

22. But lest we be dismayed by the consciousness of our native weakness and grow faint when confronted with the unattainable example which Christ, who is Man and at the same time God, has given, along with mysteries which portray Him, we have before our eyes for contemplation the mysteries of His most holy Mother.

23. She was born, it is true, of the royal family of David, but she fell heir to none of the wealth and grandeur of her ancestors. She passed her life in obscurity, in a humble town, in a home humbler still, the more content with her retirement and the poverty of her home because they left her freer to lift up her heart to God and to cling to Him closely as the supreme Goodness for which her heart yearned.

24. The Lord is with her whom He has filled with His grace and made blessed. She is designated by the heavenly messenger sent to her as the Virgin from whom, by the power of the Holy Ghost, the expected Savior of nations is to come forth clothed in our humanity. The more she wonders at the sublime dignity and gives thanks to the power and mercy of God, the more does she, conscious of no merit in

---

[28] Matthew 11:29
[29] Romans 8:35
[30] Galatians 2:20

herself, grow in humility, promptly proclaiming and consecrating herself the handmaid of God even while she becomes His Mother.

25. Her sacred promise was as sacredly kept with a joyous heart; henceforth she leads a life in perpetual union with her son Jesus, sharing with Him His joys and sorrows. It is thus that she will reach a height of glory granted to no other creature, whether human or angelic, because no one will receive a reward for virtue to be compared with hers; it is thus that the crown of the kingdoms of heaven and of earth will await her because she will be the invincible Queen of Martyrs. It is thus that she will be seated in the heavenly city of God by the side of her Son, crowned for all eternity, because she will drink with Him the cup overflowing with sorrow faithfully through all her life, most faithfully on Calvary.

26. In Mary we see how a truly good and provident God has established for us a most suitable example of every virtue. As we look upon her and think about her we are not cast down as though stricken by the overpowering splendor of God's power; but, on the contrary, attracted by the closeness of the common nature we share with her, we strive with greater confidence to imitate her. If we, with her powerful help, should dedicate ourselves wholly and entirely to the undertaking, we can portray at least an outline of such great virtue and sanctity, and reproducing that perfect conformity of our lives to all God's designs which she possessed in so marvelous a degree, we shall follow her into heaven.

27. Undaunted and full of courage, let us go on with the pilgrimage we have undertaken even though the way be rough and full of obstacle Amid the vexation and toil let us not cease to hold out suppliant hands to Mary with the words of the Church: "To thee do we send up our sigh mourning and weeping in this valley of tears; turn then, most gracious advocate, thine eyes of mercy toward us. . . Keep our lives all spotless, make our ways secure, till we find in Jesus joys that will endure." [31]

28. Although she was never subject to the frailty and perversity of our nature, Mary we knows its condition and is the best and most solicitous of mothers. How willingly will she hasten to our aid when we need her; with what love will she refresh us, and with what strength sustain us. For those of us who follow the journey hallowed by the blood of Christ and by the tears of Mary, our entrance into their company and the enjoyment of their most blessed glory will be certain and easy.

---

[31] From the Sacred Liturgy

29. Therefore the Rosary of the Blessed Virgin Mary, combining in a convenient and practical form an unexcelled form of prayer, an instrument well adapted to preserve the faith and an illustrious example of perfect virtue, should be often in the hands of the true Christian and be devoutly recited and meditated upon. We address this commendation especially to the Confraternity of the Holy Family which We recently praised and approved. Since the mystery of the hidden life which Christ our Lord long led within the walls of the house in Nazareth is the reason for the existence of this association, that its members may constantly conform themselves to Christian life on the model of the Holy Family established by God Himself, its intimate connection with the Rosary is plain.

30. Especially is this so in the joyful mysteries, which end with the one in which Jesus, after manifesting His wisdom in the temple, came with Mary and Joseph to Nazareth and was subject to them, preparing, as it were, for the other mysteries which are more closely connected with the instruction and the Redemption of mankind. From this all the members may understand that it is their duty to be devotees of the Rosary themselves and to be diligent in propagating devotion to it among others.

31. For Our part, We confirm and ratify the grants of sacred indulgences made in years past in favor of the faithful who spend the month of October in the manner We have prescribed. Because of your authority and zeal, Venerable Brethren, We know that the Catholic people will be fired with devotion and holy emulation in venerating through the Rosary, the Blessed Virgin, Help of Christians.

32. And now let Us bring Our exhortation to a close in the way it began, proclaiming once more and even more openly the devotion we cherish toward the great Mother of God, a devotion both mindful of past blessings and full of joyous hope. We ask the prayers of the Christian people in devout supplication before her altars on behalf of the Church, tormented by such adverse and turbulent times, and on behalf of Ourself as well. Advanced in age, worn out with labors, fettered by distressingly difficult events with no human help to rely upon, We must yet carry on the government of the Church. Our hope in Mary, powerful and benign Mother, is daily more confirmed and more sweetly consoling. To her intercession We attribute the many and remarkable gifts We have obtained from God; with thanks still more profuse do we attribute the fact that it has been given Us to reach the fiftieth anniversary of Our episcopal consecration.

33. It is, indeed, a great comfort to us, looking back over the long years of Our pastoral charge, troubled as they have been by daily worry, that We are still engaged in ruling the whole Christian flock. During that time We have had, as happens in men's lives and as the mysteries of Christ and Mary illustrate, reasons for joy mixed with reasons for many and bitter sorrows, as well as occasions to glory in gains won for Christ. All of this We, with a mind submissive to God and with a grateful heart, have tried to turn to the good and the honor of the Church. And now — for the rest of Our life will run a course not unlike the past — should new joys come to gladden Our heart, or sorrow to threaten Us, or honors to glory in, We, steadfast in the same heart and mind, yearning only for the heavenly glory which God confers, say with David: "Blessed be the name of the Lord"; [32] "Not to us, but to thy name give glory." [33]

34. From Our devoted children, whose filial and affectionate concern for us We know burns bright, We look for heartfelt thanks to God, prayers, and holy aspirations, rather than for congratulations and honors. It will be a special joy to Us if they ask for Us this grace, that all the strength and life that remain to Us, all the authority and grace with which We are invested, may profit the Church, and in the first place bring back into her fold her enemies and those who have wandered from the right way, to whom our voice has this long time been appealing for reconciliation.

35. Upon all of Our dearly beloved children may there flow, from the happiness and joy of Our coming Jubilee, God granting, gifts of justice, peace, prosperity, holiness, and all good things. This, with paternal love, We beg God; this do We exhort in the words of His Holy Scriptures: "Hear me. . . and bud forth as the rose planted by the brooks of waters: Give ye a sweet odor as frankincense. . . Send forth flowers, as the lily, and yield a smell, and bring forth leaves in grace and praise with canticles and bless the Lord in his works. Magnify his name, and give glory to him with the voice of your lips, and with the canticles of your mouths. and with harps. . . With the whole heart and mouth praise ye him, and bless the name of the Lord." [34]

36. If these plans, so ardently desired, be scoffed at by the wicked who blaspheme that of which they are ignorant, may God mercifully spare them. But that He may give Our hopes His propitious aid through the prayers of the Queen of the Most Holy Rosary, take as

---

[32] Psalm 112:2
[33] Psalm 113:1
[34] Ecclesiasticus 39:17-20, 41

a token of divine favor and at the same time as a pledge of Our affection, Venerable Brethren, the Apostolic Benediction, which We, lovingly in the Lord, bestow on each of you, on your clergy, and on your people.

Given at Rome, at St. Peter's, the eighth of September, 1892, in the fifteenth year of Our Pontificate.

Laetitiae Sanctae

Commending Devotion to the Rosary

To Our Venerable Brethren the Patriarchs, Primates, Archbishops, Bishops, and other Ordinaries, having Peace and Communion with the Apostolic See.

Venerable Brethren, Greeting and Apostolic Benediction.

The sacred joy which it has been given to Us to feel in attaining the fiftieth anniversary of Our Episcopal Consecration has been deepened by the knowledge that it was shared by the people of the whole Catholic world, and that as a father in the midst of his children We have been consoled by the touching testimonies of their loyalty and love. We gratefully accept it and record it as a fresh proof of God's special providence, and one which is markedly full of bounty to Ourselves, and of blessing to the Church.

2. At the same time We love to offer Our thanks for this signal benefit to the august Mother of God, whose powerful intercession We feel to have been exercised in Our behalf. For hers is the loving kindness which, during the length of years and the vicissitudes of life, has never failed Us, and which day by day seems to draw nearer to Us than ever, filling Our soul with gladness, and strengthening Us with a confidence of which the surety is higher than the things of time. It is as if the voice of the heavenly Queen made itself heard to Us, at one moment graciously consoling Us in the midst of trials; at another guiding Us by her counsel in directing the great work of the salvation of souls; at another, urging Us to admonish the Christian people to advance in piety and in the practice of every virtue. For Us it is once more a joy as well as a duty to respond to her inspirations. Amongst the happy results which have already rewarded Our exhortations which were due to her prompting, We have to reckon the remarkable impulse given to the Devotion of the Most Holy Rosary. This awakening has made itself felt in the increased number of Confraternities instituted for the purpose, the voluminous literature of pious and learned works written upon the subject, and the manifold tributes which Christian art has not failed to bring to its service. And now, as if for yet another time, listening to the voice of the same zealous Mother, who calls upon Us to "cry out and cease not," We rejoice once more to address you, Venerable Brethren, upon the subject of the Rosary, standing as We do

upon the eve of that month of October which, by the award of special Indulgences, We have deemed it well to dedicate to this most popular devotion. Our appeal to you, however, will not be directed so much to add any further recommendation of a method of prayer so praiseworthy in itself, nor yet to press upon the faithful the necessity of practising it still more fervently, but rather to point out how we may draw from this devotion certain advantages which are especially valuable and needful at the present day.

The Rosary and Society

3. For We are convinced that the Rosary, if devoutly used, is bound to benefit not only the individual but society at large. No one will do Us the injustice to deny that in the discharge of the duties of the Supreme Apostolate We have laboured - as, God helping, We shall ever continue to labour - to promote the civil prosperity of mankind. Repeatedly have We admonished those who are invested with sovereign power that they should neither make nor execute laws except in conformity with the equity of the Divine mind. On the other hand, we have constantly besought citizens who were conspicuous by genius, industry, family, or fortune, to join together in common counsel and action to safeguard and to promote whatever would tend to the strength and well-being of the community. Only too many causes are at work, in the present condition of things, to loosen the bonds of public order, and to withdraw the people from sound principles of life and conduct.

Dislike of Poverty - The Joyful Mysteries

4. There are three influences which appear to Us to have the chief place in effecting this downgrade movement of society. These are-first, the distaste for a simple and labourious life; secondly, repugnance to suffering of any kind; thirdly, the forgetfulness of the future life.

5. We deplore - and those who judge of all things merely by the light and according to the standard of nature join with Us in deploring that society is threatened with a serious danger in the growing contempt of those homely duties and virtues which make up the beauty of humble life. To this cause we may trace in the home, the readiness of children to withdraw themselves from the natural obligation of obedience to the parents, and their impatience of any form of treatment

which is not of the indulgent and effeminate kind. In the workman, it evinces itself in a tendency to desert his trade, to shrink from toil, to become discontented with his lot, to fix his gaze on things that are above him, and to look forward with unthinking hopefulness to some future equalization of property. We may observe the same temper permeating the masses in the eagerness to exchange the life of the rural districts for the excitements and pleasures of the town. Thus the equilibrium between the classes of the community is being destroyed, everything becomes unsettled, men's minds become a prey to jealousy and heart-burnings, rights are openly trampled under foot, and, finally, the people, betrayed in their expectations, attack public order, and place themselves in conflict with those who are charged to maintain it.

6. For evils such as these let us seek a remedy in the Rosary, which consists in a fixed order of prayer combined with devout meditation on the life of Christ and His Blessed Mother. Here, if the joyful mysteries be but clearly brought home to the minds of the people, an object lesson of the chief virtues is placed before their eyes. Each one will thus be able to see for himself how easy, how abundant, how sweetly attractive are the lessons to be found therein for the leading of an honest life. Let us take our stand in front of that earthly and divine home of holiness, the House of Nazareth. How much we have to learn from the daily life which was led within its walls! What an all-perfect model of domestic society! Here we behold simplicity and purity of conduct, perfect agreement and unbroken harmony, mutual respect and love - not of the false and fleeting kind - but that which finds both its life and its charm in devotedness of service. Here is the patient industry which provides what is required for food and raiment; which does so "in the sweat of the brow," which is contented with little, and which seeks rather to diminish the number of its wants than to multiply the sources of its wealth. Better than all, we find there that supreme peace of mind and gladness of soul which never fail to accompany the possession of a tranquil conscience. These are precious examples of goodness, of modesty, of humility, of hard-working endurance, of kindness to others, of diligence in the small duties of daily life, and of other virtues, and once they have made their influence felt they gradually take root in the soul, and in course of time fail not to bring about a happy change of mind and conduct. Then will each one begin to feel his work to be no longer lowly and irksome, but grateful and lightsome, and clothed with a certain joyousness by his sense of duty in discharging it conscientiously. Then will gentler manners everywhere prevail; home-life will be loved and esteemed,

and the relations of man with man will be loved and esteemed, and the relations of man with man will be hallowed by a larger infusion of respect and charity. And if this betterment should go forth from the individual to the family and to the communities, and thence to the people at large so that human life should be lifted up to this standard, no one will fail to feel how great and lasting indeed would be the gain which would be achieved for society.

Repugnance to Suffering-The Sorrowful Mysteries

7. A second evil, one which is specially pernicious, and one which, owing to the increasing mischief which it works among souls, we can never sufficiently deplore, is to be found in repugnance to suffering and eagerness to escape whatever is hard or painful to endure. The greater number are thus robbed of that peace and freedom of mind which remains the reward of those who do what is right undismayed by the perils or troubles to be met with in doing so. Rather do they dream of a chimeric civilization in which all that is unpleasant shall be removed, and all that is pleasant shall be supplied. By this passionate and unbridled desire of living a life of pleasure, the minds of men are weakened, and if they do not entirely succumb, they become demoralized and miserably cower and sink under the hardships of the battle of life.

8. In such a contest example is everything, and a powerful means of renewing our courage will undoubtedly be found in the Holy Rosary, if from our earliest years our minds have been trained to dwell upon the sorrowful mysteries of Our Lord's life, and to drink in their meaning by sweet and silent meditation. In them we shall learn how Christ, "the Author and Finisher of Our faith," began "to do and teach," in order that we might see written in His example all the lessons that He Himself had taught us for the bearing of our burden of labour and sorrow, and mark how the sufferings which were hardest to bear were those which He embraced with the greatest measure of generosity and good will. We behold Him overwhelmed with sadness, so that drops of blood ooze like sweat from His veins. We see Him bound like a malefactor, subjected to the judgment of the unrighteous, laden with insults, covered with shame, assailed with false accusations, torn with scourges, crowned with thorns, nailed to the cross, accounted unworthy to live, and condemned by the voice of the multitude as deserving of death. Here, too, we contemplate the grief of the most Holy Mother, whose soul was not merely wounded but "pierced" by

the sword of sorrow, so that she might be named and become in truth "the Mother of Sorrows." Witnessing these examples of fortitude, not with sight but by faith, who is there who will not feel his heart grow warm with the desire of imitating them?

9. Then, be it that the "earth is accursed" and brings forth "thistles and thorns,"- be it that the soul is saddened with grief and the body with sickness; even so, there will be no evil which the envy of man or the rage of devils can invent, nor calamity which can fall upon the individual or the community, over which we shall not triumph by the patience of suffering. For this reason it has been truly said that "it belongs to the Christian to do and to endure great things," for he who deserves to be called a Christian must not shrink from following in the footsteps of Christ. But by this patience, We do not mean that empty stoicism in the enduring of pain which was the ideal of some of the philosophers of old, but rather do We mean that patience which is learned from the example of Him, who "having joy set before Him, endured the cross, despising the shame" (Heb. xvi., 2). It is the patience which is obtained by the help of His grace; which shirks not a trial because it is painful, but which accepts it and esteems it as a gain, however hard it may be to undergo. The Catholic Church has always had, and happily still has, multitudes of men and women, in every rank and condition of life, who are glorious disciples of this teaching, and who, following faithfully in the path of Christ, suffer injury and hardship for the cause of virtue and religion. They re-echo, not with their lips, but with their life, the words of St. Thomas: "Let us also go, that we may die with him" (John xi., 16).

10. May such types of admirable constancy be more and more splendidly multiplied in our midst to the weal of society and to the glory and edification of the Church of God!

Forgetfulness of the Future - The Glorious Mysteries

11. The third evil for which a remedy is needed is one which is chiefly characteristic of the times in which we live. Men in former ages, although they loved the world, and loved it far too well, did not usually aggravate their sinful attachment to the things of earth by a contempt of the things of heaven. Even the right-thinking portion of the pagan world recognized that this life was not a home but a dwelling-place, not our destination, but a stage in the journey. But men of our day, albeit they have had the advantages of Christian instruction, pursue the false goods of this world in such wise that the

thought of their true Fatherland of enduring happiness is not only set aside, but, to their shame be it said, banished and entirely erased from their memory, notwithstanding the warning of St. Paul, "We have not here a lasting city, but we seek one which is to come". [35]

12. When We seek out the causes of this forgetfulness, We are met in the first place by the fact that many allow themselves to believe that the thought of a future life goes in some way to sap the love of our country, and thus militates against the prosperity of the commonwealth. No illusion could be more foolish or hateful. Our future hope is not of a kind which so monopolizes the minds of men as to withdraw their attention from the interests of this life. Christ commands us, it is true, to seek the Kingdom of God, and in the first place, but not in such a manner as to neglect all things else. For, the use of the goods of the present life, and the righteous enjoyment which they furnish, may serve both to strengthen virtue and to reward it. The splendour and beauty of our earthly habitation, by which human society is ennobled, may mirror the splendour and beauty of our dwelling which is above. Therein we see nothing that is not worthy of the reason of man and of the wisdom of God. For the same God who is the Author of Nature is the Author of Grace, and He willed not that one should collide or conflict with the other, but that they should act in friendly alliance, so that under the leadership of both we may the more easily arrive at that immortal happiness for which we mortal men were created.

13. But men of carnal mind, who love nothing but themselves, allow their thoughts to grovel upon things of earth until they are unable to lift them to that which is higher. For, far from using the goods of time as a help towards securing those which are eternal, they lose sight altogether of the world which is to come, and sink to the lowest depths of degradation. We may doubt if God could inflict upon man a more terrible punishment than to allow him to waste his whole life in the pursuit of earthly pleasures, and in forgetfulness of the happiness which alone lasts for ever.

14. It is from this danger that they will be happily rescued, who, in the pious practice of the Rosary, are wont, by frequent and fervent prayer, to keep before their minds the glorious mysteries. These mysteries are the means by which in the soul of a Christian a most clear light is shed upon the good things, hidden to sense, but visible to faith, "which God has prepared for those who love Him." From them we learn that death is not an annihilation which ends all

---

[35] Hebrews 13:4

things, but merely a migration and passage from life to life. By them we are taught that the path to Heaven lies open to all men, and as we behold Christ ascending thither, we recall the sweet words of His promise, "I go to prepare a place for you." By them we are reminded that a time will come when "God will wipe away every tear from our eyes," and that "neither mourning, nor crying, nor sorrow, shall be any more," and that "We shall be always with the Lord," and "like to the Lord, for we shall see Him as He is," and "drink of the torrent of His delight," as "fellow-citizens of the saints," in the blessed companionship of our glorious Queen and Mother. Dwelling upon such a prospect, our hearts are kindled with desire, and we exclaim, in the words of a great saint, "How vile grows the earth when I look up to heaven!" Then, too, shall we feel the solace of the assurance "that which is at present momentary and light of our tribulation worketh for us above measure exceedingly an eternal weight of glory." [36]

15. Here alone we discover the true relation between time and eternity, between our life on earth and our life in heaven; and it is thus alone that are formed strong and noble characters. When such characters can be counted in large numbers, the dignity and well-being of society are assured. All that is beautiful, good, and true will flourish in the measure of its conformity to Him who is of all beauty, goodness, and truth the first Principle and the Eternal Source.

Confraternities of the Rosary

16. These considerations will explain what We have already laid down concerning the fruitful advantages which are to be derived from the use of the Rosary, and the healing power which this devotion possesses for the evils of the age and the fatal sores of society. These advantages, as we may readily conceive, will be secured in a higher and fuller measure by those who band themselves together in the sacred Confraternity of the Rosary, and who are thus more than others united by a special and brotherly bond of devotion to the Most Holy Virgin. In this Confraternity, approved by the Roman Pontiffs, and enriched by them with indulgences and privileges, they possess their own rule and government, hold their meetings at stated times, and are provided with ample means of leading a holy life and of labouring for the good of the community. They are, are so to speak, the battalions who fight the battle of Christ, armed with His Sacred Mysteries, and under the banner and guidance of the Heavenly queen. How faithfully

---

[36] II Corinthians 4:17

her intercession is exercised in response to their prayers, processions, and solemnities is written in the whole experience of the Church not less than in the splendour of the victory of Lepanto.

17. It is, therefore, to be desired that renewed zeal should be called forth in the founding, enlarging, and directing of these confraternities, and that not only by the sons of St. Dominic, to whom by virtue of their Order a leading part in this Apostolate belongs, but by all who are charged with the care of souls, and notable in those places in which the Confraternity has not yet been canonically established. We have it especially at heart that those who are engaged in the sacred field of the missions, whether in carrying the Gospel to barbarous nations abroad, or in spreading it amongst the Christian nations at home, should look upon this work as especially their own. If they will make it the subject of their preaching, We cannot doubt that there will be large numbers of the faithful of Christ who will readily enrol themselves in the Confraternity, and who will earnestly endeavour to avail themselves of those spiritual advantages of which We have spoken, and in which consist the very meaning and motive of the Rosary. From the Confraternities, the rest of the faithful will receive the example of greater esteem and reverence for the practice of the Rosary, and they will be thus encouraged to reap from it, as We heartily desire that they may, the same abundant fruits for their souls' salvation.

Conclusion

18. This then is the hope, which, amid the manifold evils which beset society, brightens, consoles, and supports Us. May Mary, the Mother of God and of men, herself the authoress and teacher of the Rosary, procure for Us its happy fulfilment. It will be your part, Venerable Brethren, to provide that by your efforts Our words and Our wishes may go forth on their mission of good for the prosperity of families and the peace of peoples.

19. And as a pledge of the Divine favour, and of Our own affection, We lovingly bestow upon you, your clergy, and your people, the Apostolic Benediction.

Given at St. Peter's, Rome, this 8th day of September, in the year of Our Lord 1893, and the 16th of Our Pontificate.

Jucunda Semper Expectatione

ON THE ROSARY

To the Patriarchs, Primates, Archbishops, Bishops, and other Ordinaries in Peace and Communion with the Apostolic See.

Venerable Brethren, Greeting and Apostolic Benediction.

It is always with joyful expectation and inspired hope that We look forward to the return of the month of October. At Our exhortation and by Our express order this month has been consecrated to the Blessed Virgin, during which for some years now the devotion of her Rosary has been practised by Catholic nations throughout the world with sedulous earnestness. Our reasons for making this exhortation We have made known more than once. For as the disastrous condition of the Church and of Society proved to Us the extreme necessity for signal aid from God, it was manifest to Us that aid should be sought through the intercession of His Mother, and by the express means of the Rosary, which Christians have ever found to be of marvellous avail. This indeed has been well proved since the very institution of the devotion, both in the vindication of Holy Faith against the furious attacks of heresy, and in restoring to honour the virtues, which by reason of the Age's corruption, required to be rekindled and sustained. And this same proof was continued in all succeeding ages, by a never failing series of private and public benefits, whereof the illustrious remembrance is everywhere perpetuated and immortalized by monuments and existing institutions. Likewise in Our age, afflicted with that tempest of various evils, it is a joy to Our soul to relate the beneficent influence of the Rosary. Notwithstanding all this, you yourselves, Venerable Brethren, behold with your own eyes the persistence - nay, the increase - of the reasons for renewing again this year Our summons to the Faithful to turn with increased ardour in prayer to Mary, the Queen of Heaven. Besides, the more We fix Our thoughts upon the character of the Rosary, the clearer its excellence and power appear to Us. Hence, while Our wish increases that it may flourish, Our hope grows also that through Our recommendation it may come to be more greatly prized, its holy use become more extended and flourish abundantly. But We shall not now return to the various instructions which in past years We have given upon this subject. We shall take instead the opportunity of pointing out the particular ruling and designs of Providence which ordains that the Rosary should have new power to instil confidence into the hearts of those who pray, and new influence to move the compassionate heart of Our Mother to comfort and succour Us with the utmost bounty.

2. The recourse we have to Mary in prayer follows upon the office she continuously fills by the side of the throne of God as Mediatrix of Divine grace; being by worthiness and by merit most acceptable to Him, and, therefore, surpassing in power all the angels and saints in Heaven. Now, this merciful office of hers, perhaps, appears in no other form of prayer so manifestly as it does in the Rosary. For in the Rosary all the part that Mary took as our co-Redemptress comes to us, as it were, set forth, and in such wise as though the facts were even then taking place; and this with much profit to our piety, whether in the contemplation of the succeeding sacred mysteries, or in the prayers which we speak and repeat with the lips. First come the Joyful Mysteries. The Eternal Son of God stoops to mankind, putting on its nature; but with the assent of Mary, who conceives Him by the Holy Ghost. Then St. John the Baptist, by a singular privilege, is sanctified in his mother's womb and favoured with special graces that he might prepare the way of the Lord; and this comes to pass by the greeting of Mary who had been inspired to visit her cousin. At last the expected of nations comes to light, Christ the Saviour. The Virgin bears Him. And when the Shepherds and the wise men, first-fruits of the Christian faith, come with longing to His cradle, they find there the young Child, with Mary, His Mother. Then, that He might before men offer Himself as a victim to His Heavenly Father, He desires to be taken to the Temple; and by the hands of Mary He is there presented to the Lord. It is Mary who, in the mysterious losing of her Son, seeks Him sorrowing, and finds Him again with joy. And the same truth is told again in the sorrowful mysteries.

3. In the Garden of Gethsemane, where Jesus is in an agony; in the judgment-hall, where He is scourged, crowned with thorns, condemned to death, not there do we find Mary. But she knew beforehand all these agonies; she knew and saw them. When she professed herself the handmaid of the Lord for the mother's office, and when, at the foot of the altar, she offered up her whole self with her Child Jesus-then and thereafter she took her part in the laborious expiation made by her Son for the sins of the world. It is certain, therefore, that she suffered in the very depths of her soul with His most bitter sufferings and with His torments. Moreover, it was before the eyes of Mary that was to be finished the Divine Sacrifice for which she

had borne and brought up the Victim. As we contemplate Him in the last and most piteous of those Mysteries, there stood by the Cross of Jesus His Mother, who, in a miracle of charity, so that she might receive us as her sons, offered generously to Divine Justice her own Son, and died in her heart with Him, stabbed with the sword of sorrow.

4. Thence the Rosary takes us on to the Glorious Mysteries, wherein likewise is revealed the mediation of the great Virgin, still more abundant in fruitfulness. She rejoices in heart over the glory of her Son triumphant over death, and follows Him with a mother's love in His Ascension to His eternal kingdom; but, though worthy of Heaven, she abides a while on earth, so that the infant Church may be directed and comforted by her "who penetrated, beyond all belief, into the deep secrets of Divine wisdom" (St. Bernard). Nevertheless, for the fulfilment of the task of human redemption there remains still the coming of the Holy Ghost, promised by Christ. And behold, Mary is in the room, and there, praying with the Apostles and entreating for them with sobs and tears, she hastens for the Church the coming of the Spirit, the Comforter, the supreme gift of Christ, the treasure that will never fail. And later, without measure and without end will she be able to plead our cause, passing upon a day to the life immortal. Therefore we behold her taken up from this valley of tears into the heavenly Jerusalem, amid choirs of Angels. And we honour her, glorified above all the Saints, crowned with stars by her Divine Son and seated at His side the sovereign Queen of the universe.

5. If in all this series of Mysteries, Venerable Brethren, are developed the counsels of God in regard to us - "counsels of wisdom and of tenderness" (St. Bernard) - not less apparent is the greatness of the benefits for which we are debtors to the Virgin Mother. No man can meditate upon these without feeling a new awakening in his heart of confidence that he will certainly obtain through Mary the fulness of the mercies of God. And to this end vocal prayer chimes well with the Mysteries. First, as is meet and right, comes the Lord's Prayer, addressed to Our Father in Heaven: and having, with the elect petitions dictated by Our Divine Master, called upon the Father, from the throne of His Majesty we turn our prayerful voices to Mary. Thus is confirmed that law of merciful meditation of which We have spoken, and which St. Bernardine of Siena thus expresses: "Every grace granted to man has three degrees in order; for by God it is communicated to Christ, from Christ it passes to the Virgin, and from the Virgin it descends to us." And we, by the very form of the Rosary, do linger longest, and, as it were, by preference upon the last and

lowest of these steps, repeating by decades the Angelic Salutation, so that with greater confidence we may thence attain to the higher degrees-that is, may rise, by means of Christ, to the Divine Father. For if thus we again and again greet Mary, it is precisely that our failing and defective prayers may be strengthened with the necessary confidence; as though we pledged her to pray for us, and as it were in our name, to God.

6. Nor can our prayers fail to ascend to Him as a sweet savour, commended by the prayers of the Virgin. And He it is who, all-benign, invites her: "Let thy voice sound in My ears, for thy voice is sweet." For this cause do we repeatedly celebrate those glorious titles of her ministry as Mediatrix. Her do we greet who found favour with God, and who was in a signal manner filled with grace by Him so that the superabundance thereof might overflow upon all men; her, united with the Lord by the most intimate of all conjunction; her who was blessed among women, and who "alone took away the curse and bore the blessing" (St. Thomas)-that fruit of her womb, that happy fruit, in which all the nations of the earth are blessed. Her do we invoke, finally, as Mother of God; and in virtue of a dignity so sublime what graces from her may we not promise to ourselves, sinners, in life and in the agonies of the end?

7. A soul that shall devoutly repeat these prayers, that shall ponder with faith these mysteries, will, without doubt, be filled with wonder at the Divine purposes in this great Virgin and in the work of the restoration of mankind. Doubtless, this soul, moved by the warmth of love for her and of confidence, will desire to take refuge upon her breast, as was the sweet feeling of St. Bernard: "Remember, O most pious Virgin Mary, that never was it heard that any who fled to thy protection, called upon thy help, and sought thy intercession, was left forsaken." But the fruits of the Rosary appear likewise, and with equal greatness, in the turning with mercy of the heart of the Mother of God towards us. How sweet a happiness must it be for her to see us all intent upon the task of weaving crowns for her of righteous prayers and lovely praises! And if, indeed, by those prayers we desire to render to God the glory which is His due; if we protest that we seek nothing whatsoever except the fulfilment in us of His holy will; if we magnify His goodness and graciousness; if we call Him Our Father; if we, being most unworthy, yet entreat of Him His best blessings - Oh, how shall Mary in all these things rejoice! How shall she magnify the Lord! There is no language so fit to lead us to the majesty of God as the language of the Lord's Prayer. Furthermore, to each of these things for

which we pray, things that are righteous and are ordered, and are in harmony with Christian faith, hope, and charity, is added a special joy for the Blessed Virgin. With our voices she seems to hear also the voice of her Divine Son, Who with His own mouth taught us this prayer, and by His own authority commanded it, saying: "You shall pray thus." And seeing how we observe that command, saying our Rosary, she will bend towards us with the more loving solicitude; and the mystical crowns we offer her will be to her welcome, and to us fruitful of graces. And of this generosity of Mary to our supplications we have no slight pledge in the very nature of a practice that has the power to help us in praying well. In many ways, indeed, is man apt, by his frailty, to allow his thoughts to wander from God and to let his purpose go astray. But the Rosary, if rightly considered, will be found to have in itself special virtues, whether for producing and continuing a state of recollection, or for touching the conscience for its healing, or for lifting up the soul. As all men know, it is composed of two parts, distinct but inseparable-the meditation of the Mysteries and the recitation of the prayers. It is thus a kind of prayer that requires not only some raising of the soul to God, but also a particular and explicit attention, so that by reflection upon the things to be contemplated, impulses and resolutions may follow for the reformation and sanctification of life.

8. Those same things are, in fact, the most important and the most admirable of Christianity, the things through which the world was renewed and filled with the fruits of truth, justice, and peace. And it is remarkable how well adapted to every kind of mind, however unskilled, is the manner in which these things are proposed to us in the Rosary. They are proposed less as truths or doctrines to be speculated upon than as present facts to be seen and perceived. Thus presented, with the circumstances of place, time, and persons, these Mysteries produce the most living effect; and this without the slightest effort of imagination; for they are treated as things learnt and engraven in the heart from infancy. Thus, hardly is a Mystery named but the pious soul goes through it with ease of thought and quickness of feeling, and gathers therefrom, by the gift of Mary, abundance of the food of Heaven. And yet another title of joy and of acceptation in her eyes do our crowns of prayer acquire. For every time that we look once more with devotional remembrance upon these Mysteries we give her a sign of the gratitude of our hearts; we prove to her that we cannot often enough call to mind the blessings of her unwearied charity in the work of our salvation. At such recollections, practised by us with the

frequency of love in her presence, who may express, who may even conceive, what ever-new joys overflow her ever-blessed soul, and what tender affections arise therein, of mercy and of a mother's love! Besides these recollections, moreover, as the sacred Mysteries pass by they cause our prayers to be transformed into impulses of entreaty that have an indescribable power over the heart of Mary. Yes, we fly to thee, we miserable children of Eve, O holy Mother of God. To thee we lift our prayers, for thou art the Mediatrix, powerful at once and pitiful, of our salvation. Oh, by the sweetness of the joys that came to thee from thy Son Jesus, by thy participation in His ineffable sorrows, by the splendours of His glory shining in thee, we instantly beseech thee, listen, be pitiful, hear us, unworthy though we be!

9. Thus the excellence of the Rosary; considered under the double aspect We have here set forth, will convince you, Venerable Brethren, of the reasons We have for an incessant eagerness to commend and to promote it. At the present day - and on this We have already touched there is a signal necessity of special help from Heaven, particularly manifest in the many tribulations suffered by the Church as to her liberties and her rights, as also in the perils whereby the prosperity and peace of Christian society are fundamentally threatened. So it is that it belongs to Our office to assert once again that We place the best of Our hopes in the holy Rosary, inasmuch as more than any other means it can impetrate from God the succour which We need. It is Our ardent wish that this devotion shall be restored to the place of honour; in the city and in the village, in the family and in the workshop, in the noble's house and in the peasant's; that it should be to all a dear devotion and a noble sign of their faith; that it may be a sure way to the gaining of the favour of pardon. To this end it is indispensable that zeal should be redoubled, while impiety daily redoubles its efforts and labours to move the justice of God and to provoke, for the general ruin, His terrible vengeance. Amongst so many causes of grief to all good men, and to Ourself, not the least is this, that in the very midst of Catholic nations there exist persons who are ever ready to rejoice in that which insults and outrages our august religion; and that they themselves, with incredible effrontery and with all publicity, seize every opportunity of teaching the multitude to hold reverend things in contempt and of persuading them from their old confidence in the intercession of the Blessed Virgin. During the last months the very person of Our Divine Redeemer has not been spared. Such a depth of shameless indignity has been reached that Jesus Christ Himself has been dragged upon the

stage of a theatre often contaminated with corruptions, and has been represented there discrowned of that Divinity upon which rests the whole work of human salvation. And the last touch of shame was added in an attempt to rescue from the execration of ages the guilty name of him who was the very sign of perfidy, the betrayer of Christ. At the consummation of such excesses in the cities of Italy there arose a general cry of indignation, and energetic protest against the violation and trampling under foot of the inviolable rights of religion, and this in a nation that has for its greatest and most righteous boast that it is Catholic. The Bishops rose at once, on fire with holy zeal. And first they made their vigorous appeal to those whose sacred duty it is to safeguard the decorum of the religion of the country. Next, they informed their people of the gravity of the scandal, and exhorted them to special acts of reparation towards our most loving Saviour exposed to such slanders.

10. We have pleasure, however, in rendering praise to the free and fruitful faith manifested by men of good will; and this has brought Us comfort in the bitterness inflicted upon the very quick of Our heart. And having regard to the duties of Our supreme ministry, We take this occasion to lift up Our voice and to unite Our complaints and protests to those of the Bishops and of their people, authenticated by Our Apostolic authority. And with a like ardour to that wherewith we condemned this sacrilegious offence, do We preach faith to all Catholics, and particularly to the Italians. Let them with jealous care guard this inestimable inheritance received from their fathers, let them defend it with courage, let them not cease from magnifying it with good actions of which their faith is the inspiring motive. This is a motive the more for the enkindling, in private and in common prayer, throughout the coming month of October, of a holy emulation in celebrating and honouring the Mother of God, the mighty succourer of the Christian people, the most glorious Queen of Heaven. For Our own part, We confirm with all Our heart the favours and indulgences We have already awarded upon this point.

11. Now may God, "Who in His most merciful Providence gave us this Mediatrix," and "decreed that all good should come to us by the hands of Mary" (St. Bernard), receive propitiously our common prayers and fulfil our common hopes. May you receive a pledge thereof in the Apostolic Benediction which We give to you, to your clergy, and to your people, with all affection in Our Lord.

Given in Rome at St. Peter's, on September 8, 1894, in the seventeenth year of our Pontificate.

Adjutricem

On the Rosary
Pope Leo XIII - September 5, 1895
To Our Venerable Brethren the Patriarchs, Primates, Archbishops, Bishops, and other Ordinaries in Peace and Communion with the Apostolic See.

1. The mightiest helper of the Christian people, and the most merciful, is the Virgin Mother of God. How fitting it is to accord her honors ever increasing in splendor, and call upon her aid with a confidence daily growing more ardent. The abundant blessings, infinitely varied and constantly multiplying, which flow from her all over the whole world for the common benefit of mankind, add fresh motives for invoking and honoring her.

2. For such magnanimous favors, Catholics on their part have not failed to return to her the tender devotion of grateful hearts; because, if ever there was a time when love and veneration of the Blessed Virgin were awakened to new life and inflaming every class of society, it is in these days so bitterly anti-religious. The clearest evidence of this fact lies in the sodalities which have everywhere been restored and multiplied under her patronage; in the magnificent temples erected to her august name; in the pilgrimages undertaken by throngs of devout souls to her most venerated shrines; in the congresses whose deliberations are devoted to the increase of her glory; in other things of a like nature which are praiseworthy in themselves and augur well for the future.

3. It is specially deserving of notice, and it gives Us the greatest pleasure to recall, that of all the forms of devotion to the Blessed Virgin, that most excellent method of prayer, Mary's Rosary, is establishing itself most widely in popular esteem and practice. This, We repeat, is a source of great joy to Us. If We have spent so large a share of our activities, in promoting the Rosary devotion, We can easily see with what benevolence the Queen of Heaven has come to Our aid when We prayed to her; and We express the confident conviction that she will continue to stand at Our side to lighten the burdens and the afflictions which the days to come will bring.

4. It is mainly to expand the kingdom of Christ that We look to the Rosary for the most effective help. On many occasions We have declared that the object which at the present time engrosses Our most earnest attention, is the reconciliation to the Church of nations which

have become separated from her. We recognize, at the same time, that the realization of Our hopes must be sought chiefly in prayer and supplication addressed to almighty God. This conviction We again affirmed not long ago, when We recommended that special prayers be offered for this intention to the Holy Ghost during the solemnities of Pentecost; a recommendation that was adopted everywhere with the greatest good will.

5. But in view of the importance and the difficulty of such an undertaking, and the necessity of perseverance in the practice of any virtue, it is well to recall the Apostle's apt counsel: "Be instant in prayer" [37] -counsel all the more to the point because an auspicious beginning of the enterprise will supply the best inducement to perseverance in prayer. Next October, therefore, if you and your people devoutly spend the whole month with Us in praying assiduously to the Virgin Mother of God through her Rosary and the other customary devotions, nothing could do more to further this project or be more pleasing to Us. We have the best reasons for entrusting Our plans and Our aspirations to her protection and the highest hopes of seeing them realized.

6. The mystery of Christ's immense love for us is revealed with dazzling brilliance in the fact that the dying Saviour bequeathed His Mother to His disciple John in the memorable testament: "Behold thy son." Now in John, as the Church has constantly taught, Christ designated the whole human race, and in the first rank are they who are joined with Him by faith. It is in this sense that St. Anselm of Canterbury says: "What dignity, O Virgin, could be more highly prized than to be the Mother of those to whom Christ deigned to be Father and Brother!" [38] With a generous heart Mary undertook and discharged the duties of her high but laborious office, the beginnings of which were consecrated in the Cenacle. With wonderful care she nurtured the first Christians by her holy example, her authoritative counsel, her sweet consolation, her fruitful prayers. She was, in very truth, the Mother of the Church, the Teacher and Queen of the Apostles, to whom, besides, she confided no small part of the divine mysteries which she kept in her heart.

7. It is impossible to measure the power and scope of her offices since the day she was taken up to that height of heavenly glory in the company of her Son, to which the dignity and luster of her merits entitle her. From her heavenly abode she began, by God's

---

[37] Colossians 4:2
[38] Saint Ambrose Oration 47

decree, to watch over the Church, to assist and befriend us as our Mother; so that she who was so intimately associated with the mystery of human salvation is just as closely associated with the distribution of the graces which for all time will flow from the Redemption.

8. The power thus put into her hands is all but unlimited. How unerringly right, then, are Christian souls when they turn to Mary for help as though impelled by an instinct of nature, confidently sharing with her their future hopes and past achievements, their sorrows and joys, commending themselves like children to the care of a bountiful mother. How rightly, too, has every nation and every liturgy without exception acclaimed her great renown, which has grown greater with the voice of each succeeding century. Among her many other titles we find her hailed as "our Lady, our Mediatrix," [39] "the Reparatrix of the whole world," [40] "the Dispenser of all heavenly gifts." [41]

9. Since faith is the foundation, the source, of the gifts of God by which man is raised above the order of nature and is endowed with the dispositions requisite for life eternal, we are in justice bound to recognize the hidden influence of Mary in obtaining the gift of faith and its salutary cultivation-of Mary who brought the "author of faith" [42] into this world and who, because of her own great faith, was called "blessed." "O Virgin most holy, none abounds in the knowledge of God except through thee; none, O Mother of God, attains salvation except through thee; none receives a gift from the throne of mercy except through thee." [43]

10. It is no exaggeration to say that it is due chiefly to her leadership and help that the wisdom and teachings of the Gospel spread so rapidly to all the nations of the world in spite of the most obstinate difficulties and most cruel persecutions, and brought everywhere in their train a new reign of justice and peace. This it was that stirred the soul of St. Cyril of Alexandria to the following prayerful address to the Blessed Virgin: "Through you the Apostles have preached salvation to the nations. . . through you the priceless Cross is everywhere honored and venerated; through you the demons have been put to rout and mankind has been summoned back to Heaven; through you every misguided creature held in the thrall of idols is led to recognize the truth; through you have the faithful been

---

[39] Saint Bernard Sermon 2 for Advent
[40] Saint Thrasius Oration on the Assumption
[41] From the Greek Office for December 8th
[42] Hebrews 12:1
[43] Saint Germanius of Constantinople Oration 11

brought to the laver of holy Baptism and churches been founded among every people."[44]

11. Nay she has even, as this same Doctor claims, upheld and given strength to the "sceptre of the orthodox faith." [45] It has been her unremitting concern to see to it that the Catholic Faith stands firmly lodged in the midst of the people, there to thrive in its fertile and undivided unity. Many and well known are the proofs of her solicitude, manifested from time to time even in a miraculous manner. In the times and places in which, to the Church's grief, faith languished in lethargic indifference or was tormented by the baneful scourge of heresy, our great and gracious Lady in her kindness was ever ready with her aid and comfort.

12. Under her inspiration, strong with her might, great men were raised up-illustrious for their sanctity no less than for their apostolic spirit-to beat off the attacks of wicked adversaries and to lead souls back into the virtuous ways of Christian life, firing them with a consuming love of the things of God. One such man, an army in himself, was Dominic Guzman. Putting all his trust in our Lady's Rosary, he set himself fearlessly to the accomplishment of both these tasks with happy results.

13. No one will fail to remark how much the merits of the venerable Fathers and Doctors of the Church, who spent their lives in the defense and explanation of the Catholic Faith, redound to the Virgin Mother of God. For from her, the Seat of Divine Wisdom, as they themselves gratefully tell us, a strong current of the most sublime wisdom has coursed through their writings. And they were quick to acknowledge that not by themselves but by her have iniquitous errors been overcome. Finally, princes as well as Pontiffs, the guardians and defenders of the faith-the former by waging holy wars, the latter by the solemn decrees which they have issued- have not hesitated to call upon the name of the Mother of our God, and have found her answer powerful and propitious.

14. Hence it is that the Church and the Fathers have given expression to their joy in Mary in words whose beauty equals their truth: "Hail, voice of the Apostles forever eloquent, solid foundation of the faith,unshakable prop of the Church." [46] "Hail, thou through whom we have been enrolled as citizens of the One, Holy, Catholic and

---

[44] Saint Cyril of Alexander again Nestorius
[45] Saint Cyril of Alexander again Nestorius
[46] From the Greek Hymn

Apostolic Church." [47] "Hail, thou fountain springing forth by God's design, whose rivers flowing over in pure and unsullied waves of orthodoxy put to flight the hosts of error." [48] "Rejoice, because thou alone hast destroyed all the heresies in the world." [49]

15. The unexampled part which the Virgin most admirably played and still plays in the progress, the battles, and the triumphs of the Catholic Faith, makes it evident what God has planned for her to do. It should fill the hearts of all good people with a firm hope of obtaining those things which are now the object of our common desire. Trust Mary, implore her aid.

16. That the one self same profession of faith may unite the minds of Christian nations in peace and harmony, that the one and only bond of perfect charity may gather their hearts within its embrace-such is our prayerful hope! And may Mary, by her powerful help, bring this ardently desired gift into our possession! And remembering that her only begotten Son prayed so earnestly to His heavenly Father for the closest union among the nations whom He has called by the one Baptism to the one inheritance of salvation bought for an infinite price, will she not, for that reason, see to it that all in His marvelous light will strive as with one mind for unity? And will it not be her wish to employ her goodness and providence to console the Spouse of Christ, the Church, through her long-sustained efforts in this enterprise, as well as to bring to full perfection the boon of unity among the members of the Christian family, which is the illustrious fruit of her motherhood?

17. A token that the fulfillment of these hopes may soon be a reality is to be seen in the conviction and the confidence which warms the hearts of the devout. Mary will be the happy bond to draw together, with strong yet gentle constraint, all who love Christ, no matter where they may be, to form a nation of brothers yielding obedience to the Vicar of Christ on earth, the Roman Pontiff, their common Father.

18. Here our mind, almost of its own accord, looks back through the annals of the Church to the illustrious examples of her ancient unity, and dwells with affectionate regard on the memory of the great Council of Ephesus. The absolute unity of faith, the participation in identical worship, which in those days linked East with West, manifested itself in the Council with a strength unparalleled, and

---

[47] Saint John Damascene on the Assumption
[48] Saint Germanius of Constantinople on the Presentation
[49] In the Office of the Blessed Virgin Mary

shone beyond it with a radiant beauty when, after the Fathers had emphasized the dogma that the Blessed Virgin is the Mother of God, the news of their procedure-spread abroad from the exultant populace of that most devout of cities-filled all Christendom with transports of universal joy.

19. Every motive which bolsters and increases confidence in the power of our mighty and kindhearted Virgin Mother to obtain the things we ask for, should act as a powerful incentive generating in us that fiery zeal to pray to her-a zeal We would incite in every Catholic heart. Let each one weigh for himself, moreover, how fitting is this practice and how fruitful to himself; and how acceptable and pleasing to the Blessed Virgin it is bound to be. For, possessing as they do unity of faith, Catholics thus make clear not only that they value this precious gift at its true worth, but also that they intend to hold to it with jealous tenacity. No better way is afforded of proving a fraternal feeling toward their separated brethren than to aid them by every means within their power to recover this, the greatest of all gifts.

20. Such brotherly affection, truly Christian and practiced as long as the Church can remember, has traditionally sought a special efficacy from the Mother of God, since she has been the foremost promoter of peace and unity. St. Germain of Constantinople addresses this prayer to her: "Be mindful of Christians who are thy servants; commend the prayers of all; help all to realize their hopes; strengthen the faith; keep the Church in unity." [50] And to this day the Greeks beseech her in this manner: "O Virgin most pure, whose privilege it is to approach thy Son without fear of rebuff! Beseech Him, O Virgin most holy, to grant peace to the world and to breathe into the churches of Christendom one mind and one heart; and we shall all magnify thee." [51]

21. There is another special reason why Mary will be favorably disposed to grant our united prayers in behalf of the nations cut off from communion with the Church: namely, the prodigious things they have done for her honor in the past, especially in the East. To them is due much of the credit for propagating and increasing devotion to her. From them have come some of the best-remembered heralds and champions of her dignity, who have wielded a mighty influence by their authority or by their writings-eulogists famed for the ardor and the charm of their eloquence; "empresses well beloved of God," [52] who

---

[50] Historical Oration on the Dormition of the Blessed Virgin Mary
[51] Theotokion
[52] Saint Cyril of Alexander on the Faith

imitated the Virgin most pure in the example of their lives, and paid honor to her with lavish generosity; temples and basilicas built to her glory with regal splendor.

22. And We may here add a detail not foreign to Our subject and reflecting further glory upon the Mother of God. It is common knowledge that, under the changing fortunes of time, great numbers of venerable images of our Lady have been brought from the East to the West, most of them finding their way to Italy and to Rome.

23. Our forebears received them with deepest respect and venerated them with magnificent honors; and their descendants, emulating their piety, continue to cherish these images as highly sacred treasures. It is a delight for the mind to discover in this fact the approval and the favor of a mother wholly devoted to her children. For it seems to indicate that these images have been left in our midst as witness of the ages when the entire Christian family was held together by ties of absolute unity, and as so many precious pledges of our common inheritance. The very sight of them must needs invite souls, as though the Virgin herself were bidding them, to keep in devout remembrance those whom the Catholic Church calls with loving care back to the peace and the gladness which they formerly enjoyed, within her embrace.

24. And so, in Mary, God has given us the most zealous guardian of Christian unity. There are, of course, more ways than one to win her protection by prayer, but as for Us, We think that the best and most effective way to her favor lies in the Rosary. We have elsewhere brought it to the attention of the devout Christian and not least among the advantages of the Rosary is the ready and easy means it puts in his hands to nurture his faith, and to keep him from ignorance of his religion and the danger of error.

25. The very origin of the Rosary makes that plain. When such faith is exercised by vocally repeating the Our Father and Hail Mary of the Rosary prayers, or better still in the contemplation of the mysteries, it is evident how close we are brought to Mary. For every time we devoutly say the Rosary in supplication before her, we are once more brought face to face with the marvel of our salvation; we watch the mysteries of our Redemption as though they were unfolding before our eyes; and as one follows another, Mary stands revealed at once as God's Mother and our Mother.

26. The sublimity of that double dignity, the fruits of her twofold ministry, appear in vivid light when in devout meditation we think of Mary's share in the joyful, the sorrowful, the glorious

mysteries of her Son. The heart is inflamed by these reflections with a feeling of grateful love toward her and, esteeming everything beneath her as so much worthless chaff, strives with manful purpose to prove worthy of such a Mother and the gifts she bestows. Meditation on the mysteries of the Rosary, often repeated in the spirit of faith, cannot help but please her and move her, the fondest of mothers, to show mercy to her children.

27. For that reason We say that the Rosary is by far the best prayer by which to plead before her the cause of our separated brethren. To grant a favorable hearing belongs properly to her office of spiritual Mother. For Mary has not brought forth-nor could she-those who are of Christ except in the one same Faith and in the one same love; for "Can Christ be divided?" [53] All must live the life of Christ in an organic unity in order to "bring forth fruit to God" [54] in the one same body. Every one of the multitudes, therefore, whom the mischief of calamitous events has stolen away from that unity, must be born again to Christ of that same Mother whom God has endowed with a never failing fertility to bring forth a holy people. And this Mary, for her part, longs to do. Adorned by us with garlands of her favorite prayer, she will obtain by her entreaties help in abundance from the Spirit that quickeneth. God grant that they refuse not to comply with the burning desire of their merciful Mother but, on the contrary, give ear, like men of good will, with a proper regard for their eternal salvation, to the voice, gently persuasive, which calls to them: "My little children, of whom I am in labor again, until Christ be formed in you." [55]

28. Knowing what power our Lady's Rosary possesses, not a few of Our Predecessors took special care to spread the devotion throughout the countries of the East-in particular Eugene IV in the Constitution "Advesperascente" issued in 1439, and later Innocent XII and Clement XI. By their authority, privileges of wide extent were granted to the Order of Preachers in favor of this project. The hoped-for results were forthcoming, thanks to the energetic activity of the brethren of that Order, result to which many a bright record bears witness, although time and adversity have since raised great obstacles in the way of further progress. Yet even today the same zeal for the Rosary devotion which We cited at the beginning of this Letter still fills the hearts of great numbers in those lands-a fact which, We trust,

---

[53] I Corinthians 1:13
[54] Romans 7:4
[55] Galatians 4:19

will be as useful in the realization of Our hopes as it was in raising them.

29. Along with this hope, there is the joyful fact, of equal importance to the East and the West, and in keeping with the longing We have expressed: namely the plan, Venerable Brethren, which took form at the celebrated Eucharistic Congress held in Jerusalem, to build a shrine in honor of the Queen of the Most Holy Rosary at Patras in Achaia, not far from places where at one time Christianity, under her patronage, shone brilliantly. For, as We have with great pleasure learned from the committee which was organized with Our approval to advance the project and take charge of the work, most of you have already sent in contributions collected for this purpose and have promised to continue your help until the project has been completed.

30. On the strength of this it has been decided to begin work on a scale proportioned to the size of the undertaking, and We have granted permission for the laying of the first stone of the shrine at an early date with solemn ceremonies. The temple will stand as a monument of ever lasting thanksgiving erected in the name of the Christian people to their heavenly Helper and Mother. There she will be invoked unceasingly in the Greek and the Latin rites that, ever more propitious, she will continue to heap new favors upon the ancient blessings.

31. And now, Venerable Brethren, Our exhortation returns to the point from which it began. Well may all, shepherds and flocks alike, fly with fullest confidence to the protection of the great Virgin, especially next month. Let them not fail to call upon her name, with one voice beseeching her as God's Mother, publicly and in private, by praise, by prayer, by the ardor of their desire: "Show thyself our Mother." May her motherly compassion keep her whole family safe from every danger, lead them in the path of genuine prosperity, above all establish them in holy unity. She looks upon Catholics of every nation with a kindly eye. Where the bond of charity joins them together she makes them more ready, more and more determined, to uphold the honor of religion which, at the same time, brings upon the state the greatest blessings. May she look with utmost compassion upon those great and illustrious nations which are cut off from the Church and upon the noble souls who have not forgotten their Christian duty.

32. May she aspire in them most salutary desires, foster their holy aspirations, and bring them to happy completion. In the East, may that widespread devotion to her which the dissident nations profess, as

well as the countless glorious acts of their ancestors in her honor, effectively aid them. In the West, may the memory of her beneficent patronage stand its dissidents in good stead; with surpassing kindness she has, through many ages, manifested her approval of, and has rewarded, the admirable devotion shown her among every class.

33. May the peoples of the East and West, and all the others wherever they may be, profit by the suppliant voice of Catholics united in prayer, and by our voice which will cry to Our last breath: Show thyself a Mother.

Given at Rome, at St. Peter's, the fifth day of September, in the eighteenth year of Our Pontificate.

Fidentem Piumque Animum

On the Rosary
Pope Leo XIII - September 20, 1896
To Our Venerable Brethren, The Patriarchs, Primates, Bishops, and other Local Ordinaries Enjoying Peace and Communion with the Apostolic See.

Venerable Brethren, Health and the Apostolic Blessing.

1. We have already had the opportunity on several occasions during Our Pontificate of bearing public testimony to that confidence and devotion towards the Blessed Virgin which We imbibed in Our tenderest years, and have endeavoured to cherish and develop all our life long. For, having fallen upon times of calamity for Christendom and perils for the nations, We have realised how prudent it is to warmly recommend this means of safeguarding happiness and peace which God has most mercifully granted to Mankind in His August Mother, and which hath ever been celebrated in the annals of the Church. The manifold zeal of Christian people has responded to Our desires and exhortations, most particularly in exciting a devotion to the Rosary; and a plentiful harvest of excellent fruits has not been wanting. Still we can never be satisfied with celebrating the Divine Mother, who is in truth worthy of all praise, and in urging love and affection towards her who is also the mother of mankind, who is full of mercy, full of grace. Yea, Our soul, wearied with the cares of the Apostolate, the nearer it feels the time of Our departure to be at hand, with the more earnest confidence looks up to her from whom, as from a blessed dawn, arose the Day of happiness and joy that was never to set. It is pleasant to us to remember, Venerable Brethren, that We have in other letters issued from time to time extolled the devotion of the Rosary; for it is in many ways most pleasing to her in whose honour it is employed, and most advantageous to those who properly use it. But it is equally pleasant to be able now to insist upon and confirm the same fact. Herein we have an excellent opportunity to paternally exhort men's minds and hearts to an increase of religion, and to stimulate within them the hope of eternal reward.

2. The form of prayer We refer to has obtained the special name of "Rosary," as though it represented by its arrangement the sweetness of roses and the charm of a garland. This is most fitting for a method of venerating the Virgin, who is rightly styled the Mystical

Rose of Paradise, and who, as Queen of the universe, shines therein with a crown of stars. So that by its very name it appears to foreshadow and be an augury of the joys and garlands of Heaven offered by her to those who are devoted to her. This appears clearly if we consider the nature of the Rosary of Our Lady. There is no duty which Christ and His Apostles more emphatically urged by both precept and example than that of prayer and supplication to Almighty God. The Fathers and Doctors in subsequent times have taught that this is a matter of such grave necessity, that if men neglect it they hope in vain for eternal salvation. Every one who prays finds the door open to impetration, both from the very nature of prayer and from the promises of Christ. And we all know that prayer derives its chief efficacy from two principal circumstances: perseverance, and the union of many for one end. The former is signified in those invitations of Christ so full of goodness: ask, seek, knock [56], just as a kind father desires to indulge the wishes of his children, but who also requires to be continually asked by them and as it were wearied by their prayers, in order to attach their hearts more closely to himself. The second condition Our Lord has born witness to more than once: If two of you shall consent upon earth concerning anything whatsoever they shall ask, it shall be done to them by My Father who is in heaven. For where there are two or three gathered in My name, there am I in the midst of them. [57] Hence that pregnant saying of Tertullian: Let us gather into an assembly and congregation that we may, as it were, make up a band and solicit God: such violence is pleasing to God; and the memorable words of Aquinas: It is impossible that the prayers of many should not be heard, if one prayer is made up as it were out of many supplications. Both of these qualities are conspicuous in the Rosary. For, to be brief, by repeating the same prayers we strenuously implore from Our Heavenly Father the Kingdom of His grace and glory; we again and again beseech the Virgin Mother to aid us sinners by her prayers, both during our whole life and especially at that last moment which is the stepping-stone to eternity. The formula of the Rosary, too, is excellently adapted to prayer in common, so that it has been styled, not without reason, "The Psalter of Mary." And that old custom of our forefathers ought to be preserved or else restored, according to which Christian families, whether in town or country, were religiously wont at close of day, when their labours were at an end, to assemble before a figure of Our Lady and alternately recite the Rosary. She, delighted at

---

[56] Matthew 7:7
[57] Matthew 18:19-20

this faithful and unanimous homage, was ever near them like a loving mother surrounded by her children, distributing to them the blessings of domestic peace, the foretaste of the peace of heaven. Considering the efficacy of public prayer, We, among other decrees which we have from time to time issued concerning the Rosary, have spoken thus: "It is Our desire that in the principal church of each diocese it should be recited every day, and in parish churches on every feast-day." [58] Let this be constantly and devoutly carried out. We also see with joy the custom extended on other solemn occasions of public devotion and in pilgrimages to venerated shrines, the growing frequency of which is to be commended. This association of prayer and praise to Mary is both delightful and salutary for souls. We ourselves have most strongly experienced this – and Our heart rejoices to recall it – when at certain times in Our Pontificate We have been present in the Vatican basilica, surrounded by great crowds of all classes, who united with Us in mind, voice, and hope, earnestly invoked by the mysteries and prayers of the Rosary, her who is the most powerful patroness of the Catholic name.

3. And who could think or say that the confidence so strongly felt in the patronage and protection of the Blessed Virgin is excessive? Undoubtedly the name and attributes of the absolute Mediator belong to no other than to Christ, for being one person, and yet both man and God, He restored the human race to the favour of the Heavenly Father: One Mediator of God and men, the man Christ Jesus, who gave Himself a redemption for all. [59] And yet, as the Angelic Doctor teaches, there is no reason why certain others should not be called in a certain way mediators between God and man, that is to say, in so far as they cooperate by predisposing and ministering in the union of man with God. Such are the angels and saints, the prophets and priests of both Testaments; but especially has the Blessed Virgin a claim to the glory of this title. For no single individual can even be imagined who has ever contributed or ever will contribute so much towards reconciling man with God. She offered to mankind. hastening to eternal ruin, a Saviour, at that moment when she received the announcement of the mystery of peace brought to this earth by the Angel, with that admirable act of consent in the name of the whole human race. She it is from whom is born Jesus; she is therefore truly His mother, and for this reason a worthy and acceptable "Mediatrix to the Mediator." As the various mysteries present themselves one after the other in the formula of the Rosary for the meditation and

---

[58] Apostolic Letter Salutaris Ille, 24th December, 1883
[59] I Timothy 2:5-6

contemplation of men's minds, they also elucidate what we owe to Mary for our reconciliation and salvation. No one can fail to be sweetly affected when considering her who appeared in the house of Elizabeth as the minister of the divine gifts, and who presented her Son to the Shepherds, to the kings, and to Simeon. Moreover, one must remember that the Blood of Christ shed for our sake and those members in which He offers to His Father the wounds He received, the price of our liberty, are no other than the flesh and blood of the virgin, since the flesh of Jesus is the flesh of Mary, and however much it was exalted in the glory of His resurrection, nevertheless the nature of His flesh derived from Mary remained and still remains the same.

4. Yet another excellent fruit follows from the Rosary, exceedingly opportune to the character of our times. This we have referred to elsewhere. It is that, whilst the virtue of Divine Faith is daily exposed to so many dangers and attacks, the Christian may here derive nourishment and strength for his faith. Holy writ calls Christ the Author and finisher of faith, [60] the Author, because He taught men many things which they had to believe, especially about Himself in whim dwelleth all the fullness of the Godhead (Colos. ii., 9), and also because He mercifully gives the power of believing by the grace and, as it were, the function of the Holy Ghost; the Finisher, because in Heaven, where He will change the habit of faith into the splendour of glory, He openly discloses to them those things which they have seen in this mortal life as through a veil. Now Christ stands forth clearly in the Rosary. We behold in meditation His life, whether His hidden life in joy, or His public life in excessive toil and sufferings unto death, or His glorious life from His triumphant resurrection to His eternal enthronement at the right hand of the Father. And since faith, to be full and sufficient, must display itself, – for with the heart we believe unto justice, but with the mouth confession is made unto salvation, [61] – so have we also in the Rosary an excellent means unto this, for by those vocal prayers with which it is intermingled, we are enabled to express and profess our faith in God, our most watchful Father; in the future life, the forgiveness of sins; in the mysteries of the august Trinity, the Incarnation of the Word, the Divine Maternity, and others. All know the value and merit of faith. For faith is just like a most precious gem, producing now the blossoms of all virtue by which we are pleasing to God, and hereafter to bring forth fruits that will last for ever: for to know Thee is perfect justice, and to know Thy justice and Thy power

---

[60] Hebrews 7:2
[61] Romans 10:10

is the root of immortality.[62] It is here the place to add a remark respecting the duties of those virtues which faith rightly postulates. Among them is the virtue of penance, and one part of this is abstinence, which for more reasons than one is necessary and salutary. It is true the Church is growing more indulgent towards her children in this matter, but they must understand they are bound to take all care to make up for this maternal indulgence by other good works. We rejoice for this reason also to propose particularly the use of the rosary, which is capable of producing worthy fruits of penance, especially by the remembrance of the sufferings of Christ and His Mother.

5. To those therefore who are striving after supreme happiness this means of the Rosary has been most providentially offered, and it is one unsurpassed for facility and convenience. For any person, even moderately instructed in his religion can make use of it with fruit, and the time it occupies cannot delay any man's business. Sacred history abounds with striking and evident examples. It is well known that there have been many persons occupied in most weighty functions or absorbed in laborious cares who have never omitted for a single day this pious practice. Combined with this advantage is that inward sentiment of devotion which attracts minds to the Rosary, so that they love it as the intimate companion and faithful protector of life; and in their last agony they embrace and hold fast to it as the dear pledge of the unfading Crown of glory. Such a pledge is greatly enhanced by the benefits of sacred indulgences, if properly employed; for the devotion of the Rosary has been richly endowed with such indulgences by both our Predecessors and Ourselves. These favours will certainly prove most efficacious to both the dying and the departed, being bestowed as it were by the hands of the merciful Virgin, in order that they may the sooner enjoy the eternal peace and light they have desired.

6. These considerations, Venerable Brethren, move us incessantly to extol and recommend to Catholic peoples this excellent and most salutary form of devotion. Yet another very urgent reason, of which we have often spoken both in Letters and Allocutions, encourages us to do this. For that earnest desire, which We have learnt from the Divine Heart of Jesus, of fostering the work of reconciliation among those who are separated from Us daily urges Us more pressingly to action; and we are convinced that this most excellent Re-union cannot be better prepared and strengthened than by the power of prayer. The example of Christ is before us, for in order that His disciples might be one in faith and charity, he poured forth prayer and

---

[62] Wisdom 15:3

supplication to His Father. And concerning the efficacious prayer of His most holy Mother for the same end, there is a striking testimony in the Acts of the Apostles. Therein is described the first assembly of the Disciples, expecting with earnest hope and prayer the promised fullness of the Holy Ghost. And the presence of Mary united with them in prayer is specially indicated: All these were persevering with one mind in prayer with Mary the Mother of Jesus. [63] Wherefore as the nascent church rightly joined itself in prayer with her as the patroness and most excellent custodian of Unity, so in these times is it most opportune to do the same all over the Catholic World, particularly during the whole month of October, which we have long ago decreed to be dedicated and consecrated, by the solemn devotion of the Rosary, to the Divine Mother, in order to implore her for the afflicted Church. Let then the zeal for this prayer everywhere be re-kindled, particularly for the end of Holy Unity. Nothing will be more agreeable and acceptable to Mary; for, as she is most closely united with Christ she especially wishes and desires that they who have received the same Baptism with Him may be united with Him and with one another in the same faith and perfect charity. So may the sublime mysteries of this same faith by means of the Rosary devotion be more deeply impressed in men's minds, with the happy result that "we may imitate what they contain and obtain what they promise."

7. Meanwhile, as a pledge of the Divine Favours and Our affection, We most lovingly impart to You, your clergy and People, the Apostolic Benediction.

Given at St. Peter's in Rome, September 20, 1896, in the 19th year of Our Pontificate.

---

[63] Acts 1:14

Augustissimae Virginis Mariae

On the Confraternity of the Holy Rosary
Pope Leo XIII - September 12, 1897
To Our Venerable Brethren, The Patriarchs, Primates, Archbishops, Bishops, and other Local Ordinaries having Peace and Communion with the Apostolic See.

Venerable Brethren, Health and the Apostolic Blessing.

1. Whoever considers the height of dignity and glory to which God has raised the Most August Virgin Mary, will easily perceive how important it is, both for public and for private benefit, that devotion to her should be assiduously practised, and daily promoted more and more.
2. Mary's Place in the Incarnation and Redemption 2. God predestined her from all eternity to be the Mother of the Incarnate Word, and for that reason so highly distinguished her among all His most beautiful works in the triple order of nature, grace and glory, that the Church justly applies to her these words: "I came out of the mouth of the Most High, the first-born before all creatures." [64] And when, in the first ages, the parents of mankind fell into sin, involving their posterity in the same ruin, she was set up as a pledge of the restoration of peace and salvation. The Only-begotten Son of God ever paid to His Most Holy Mother indubitable marks of honour. During His private life on earth He associated her with Himself in each of His first two miracles: the miracle of grace, when, at the salutation of Mary, the infant leaped in the womb of Elizabeth; the miracle of nature, when He turned water into wine at the marriage-feast of Cana. And, at the supreme moment of His public life, when sealing the New Testament in His precious Blood, He committed her to his beloved Apostle in those sweet words, "Behold, thy Mother!" [65]
3. We, therefore, who, though unworthy, hold the place of Vicar of Christ upon earth, shall never cease to promote the glory of so great a Mother, as long as life endures. And since, as old age draws on apace, We feel that life cannot now last much longer, We are constrained to repeat to each and all of our beloved children in Christ those last words of His upon the Cross, left to us as a testament, "Behold, thy Mother!" Greatly rewarded indeed shall We be, if Our

---
[64] Ecclesiasticus 24:5
[65] John 19:27

exhortations succeed in making even one of the faithful hold nothing dearer than devotion to Mary; so that those words which St. John wrote about himself may be applied to each,"the disciple took her to his own." [66]

4. As the month of October again approaches, Venerable Brethren, We would not willingly leave you without Our letters this year, also once more urging you with all possible earnestness to strive by the recitation of the Rosary to aid both yourselves individually, and the Church in her need. This form of prayer ap pears, under the guidance of Divine Providence, to have been wonderfully developed at the close of the century, for the purpose of stimulating the lagging piety of the faithful. This is witnessed by the splendid churches and much-frequented sanctuaries of the Mother of God. To this Divine Mother we have offered the flowers of the month of May; to her we would have also fruit-bearing October dedicated with especial tenderness of devotion. It is fitting that both parts of the year should be consecrated to her who said: "My flowers are the fruit of honour and riches." [67]

5. The natural tendency of man to association has never been stronger, or more earnestly and generally followed, than in our own age. This is not at all to be reprehended, unless when so excellent a natural tendency is perverted to evil purposes, and wicked men, banding together in various forms of societies, conspire "against the Lord and against His Christ." [68] It is, however, most gratifying to observe that pious associations are becoming more and more popular among Catholics also. They are frequently formed; indeed, all Catholics are so closely drawn together and united by the bonds of charity, as members of one household, that they both may be and are truly styled brethren. But if the charity of Christ be absent, none may glory in the name and fellowship of brethren. So wrote Tertullian long ago in pungent words: "We are your brethren by right of a common mother, nature, yet are ye less than men, because unnatural brothers. How much more justly are they called and esteemed as brethren who acknowledge one and the same Father, God; who have drunk in one and the same spirit of charity; who have been borne from one and the same womb of ignorance into the one light of truth?"

6. There are many reasons for Catholics joining useful associations of this kind. We include in these clubs, popular savings-

---

[66] John 19:27
[67] Ecclesiasticus 24:23
[68] Psalms 2:2

banks, recreative classes, associations for the care of youth, sodalities, and many other organizations for excellent purposes. All these, though from their name, constitution, and special ends, apparently of modern invention, are in reality of great antiquity. Traces of societies of this kind are to be found even in the earliest ages of Christianity. In later ages they were legally approved, distinguished by special emblems, enriched with privileges, associated with divine worship in the Churches, or devoted to works of spiritual or corporal mercy, and at different epochs known under different names. Their numbers increased to such an extent, especially in Italy, that no city or town, nay scarcely any parish, was without one or more of them.

7. We do not hesitate to assign a pre-eminent place among these societies to that known as the Society of the Holy Rosary. If we regard its origin, we find it distinguished by its antiquity, for St. Dominic himself is said to have been its founder. If we estimate its privileges, we see it enriched with a vast number of them granted by the munificence of our predecessors. The form of the association, its very soul, is the Rosary of Our Lady, of the excellence of which We have elsewhere spoken at length. Still the virtue and efficacy of the Rosary appear all the greater when considered as the special office of the Sodality which bears its name. Everyone knows how necessary prayer is for all men; not that God's decrees can be changed, but, as St. Gregory says, "that men by asking may merit to receive what Almighty God hath decreed from eternity to grant them." And St. Augustine says, "He who knoweth how to pray aright, knoweth how to live aright." But prayers acquire their greatest efficacy in obtaining God's assistance when offered publicly, by large numbers, constantly, and unanimously, so as to form as it were a single chorus of supplication; as those words of the Acts of the Apostles clearly declare wherein the disciples of Christ, awaiting the coming of the Holy Ghost, are said to have been "persevering with one mind in prayer." [69] Those who practice this manner of prayer will never fail to obtain certain fruit. Such is certainly the case with members of the Rosary Sodality. Just as by the recitation of the Divine Office, priests offer a public, constant, and most efficacious supplication; so the supplication offered by the members of this Sodality in the recitation of the Rosary, or "Psalter of Our Lady," as it has been styled by some of the Popes, is also in a way public, constant, and universal.

8. Since, as We have said, public prayers are much more excellent and more efficacious than private ones, so ecclesiastical

---
[69] Acts 1:14

writers have given to the Rosary Sodality the title of "the army of prayer, enrolled by St. Dominic, under the banner of the Mother of God," – of her, whom sacred literature and the history of the Church salute as the conqueror of the Evil One and of all errors. The Rosary unites together all who join the Sodality in a common bond of paternal or military comradeship; so that a mighty host is thereby formed, duly marshalled and arrayed, to repel the assaults of the enemy, both from within and without. Wherefore may the members of this pious society take to themselves the words of St. Cyprian: "Our prayer is public and in common; and when we pray, we pray not for one, but for the whole people, for we, the entire people, are one." The history of the Church bears testimony to the power and efficacy of this form of prayer, recording as it does the rout of the Turkish forces at the naval battle of Lepanto, and the victories gained over the same in the last century at Temesvar in Hungary and in the island of Corfu. Our predecessor, Gregory XIII, in order to perpetuate the memory of the first-named victory, established the feast of Our Lady of Victories, which later on Clement XI distinguished by the title of Rosary Sunday and commanded to be celebrated throughout the universal Church.

9. From the fact that this warfare of prayer is "enrolled under the name of the Mother of God," fresh efficacy and fresh honour are thereby added to it. Hence the frequent repetition in the Rosary of the "Hail Mary" after each "Our Father." So far from this derogating in any way from the honour due to God, as though it indicated that we placed greater confidence in Mary's patronage than in God's power, it is rather this which especially moves God, and wins His mercy for us. We are taught by the Catholic faith that we may pray not only to God himself, but also to the Blessed in heaven (Conc. Trid. Sess. xxv.), though in different manner; because we ask from God as from the Source of all good, but from the Saints as from intercessors. "Prayer," says St. Thomas, "is offered to a person in two ways – one as though to be granted by himself; another, as to be obtained through him. In the first way we pray to God alone, because all our prayers ought to be directed to obtaining grace and glory, which God alone gives, according to those words of Psalms 83:12: "The Lord will give grace and glory." But in the second way we pray to holy angels and men, not that God may learn our petition through them, but that by their prayers and merits our prayers may be efficacious. Wherefore, it is said in the Apocalypse (viii., 4): "The smoke of the incense of the prayers of the Saints ascended up before God from the hand of the angel." Now, of all the blessed in heaven, who can compare with the august Mother of

God in obtaining grace? Who seeth more clearly in the Eternal Word what troubles oppress us, what are our needs? Who is allowed more power in moving God? Who can compare with her in maternal affection? We do not pray to the Blessed in the same way as to God; for we ask the Holy Trinity to have mercy on us, but we ask all the Saints to pray for us. Yet our manner of praying to the Blessed Virgin has something in common with our worship of God, so that the Church even addresses to her the words with which we pray to God: "Have mercy on sinners." The members of the Rosary Sodality, therefore, do exceedingly well in weaving together, as in a crown, so many salutations and prayers to Mary. For, so great is her dignity, so great her favour before God, that whosoever in his need will not have recourse to her is trying to fly without wings.

10. We must not omit to mention another excellence of this Sodality. As often as, in reciting the Rosary, we meditate upon the mysteries of our Redemption, so often do we in a manner emulate the sacred duties once committed to the Angelic hosts. The Angels revealed each of these mysteries in its due time; they played a great part in them; they were constantly present at them, with countenances indicative now of joy, now of sorrow, now of triumphant exultation. Gabriel was sent to announce the Incarnation of the Eternal Word to the Virgin. In the cave of Bethlehem, Angels sang the glory of the new-born Saviour. The Angel gave Joseph command to fly with the Child into Egypt. An Angel consoled, with his loving words, Jesus in His bloody sweat in the garden. Angels announced His resurrection, after He had triumphed over death, to the women. Angels carried Him up into Heaven; and foretold His second coming, surrounded by Angelic hosts, unto whom He will associate the souls of the elect, and carry them aloft with Him to the heavenly choirs, "above whom the Holy Mother of God is exalted." To those, therefore, who make use of the pious prayers of the Rosary in this Sodality, may be well applied the words with which St. Paul addressed the new Christians: "You are come to Mount Sion, and to the city of the living God, the Heavenly Jerusalem, and to the company of many thousands of Angels." [70] What more divine, what more delightful, than to meditate and pray with the Angels? With what confidence may we not hope that those who on earth have united with the Angels in this ministry will one day enjoy their blessed company in Heaven?

11. For these reasons the Roman Pontiffs have ever given the highest praise to this Sodality of Our Lady. Innocent VIII calls it "a

---

[70] Hebrews 12:22

most devout confraternity." [71] Pius V declares that by its virtue "Christians began suddenly to be transformed into other men, the darkness of heresy to be dispelled, and the light of Catholic faith to shine forth." [72] Sixtus V, noting how fruitful for religion this Sodality was, professed himself most devoted to it. Many others, too, enriched it with numerous and very special indulgences, or took it under their particular patronage, enrolling themselves in it and giving it many testimonies of their goodwill.

    12. We also, Venerable Brethren, moved by the example of Our predecessors, earnestly exhort and conjure you, as We have so often done, to devote special care to this sacred warfare, so that by your efforts fresh forces may be daily enrolled on every side. Through you and those of your clergy who have care of souls, let the people know and duly appreciate the efficacy of this Sodality and its usefulness for man's salvation. This We beg all the more earnestly as of late that beautiful devotion to our Blessed Mother, called "the living Rosary," has once more become popular. We have gladly blessed this devotion, and We earnestly desire that you would sedulously and strenuously encourage its growth. We cherish the strongest hope that these prayers and praises, rising incessantly from the lips and hearts of so great a multitude, will be most efficacious. Alternately rising by night and by day, throughout the different countries of the earth, they combine a harmony of vocal prayer with meditation upon the divine mysteries. In ages long past this perennial stream of praise and prayer was foretold in those inspired words with which Ozias in his song addressed Judith: "Blessed art thou, O daughter, by the Lord, the Most High God, above all women upon the earth . . . because He hath so magnified thy name this day that thy praise shall not depart out of the mouth of man." And all the people of Israel acclaimed him in these words: "So be it, so be it!" [73]

    13. Meanwhile, as a pledge of heavenly blessings, and a testimony of Our paternal affection, We lovingly impart to You, in the name of the Lord, Venerable Brethren, and to all the clergy and people committed to your faithful care, the Apostolic Benediction.

    Given at St. Peter's, in Rome, on the 12th day of September, 1897, in the 20th year of Our Pontificate.

---

[71] Splendor Paternae Gloriae, Feb. 26, 1491
[72] Consueverunt Romani Pontifices, September 17, 1569
[73] Judith 13;23,24,26

Diuturni Temporis

On the Rosary
Pope Leo XIII - September 5, 1898
To Our Venerable Brethren, the Patriarchs, Primates, Archbishops, Bishops, and other Local Ordinaries having Peace and Communion with the Apostolic See.

Venerable Brethren, Health and Apostolic Benediction.

1. Looking back over the long space of time, which by God's Will We have passed in the Supreme Pontificate, We cannot but acknowledge that, in spite of Our demerits, We have enjoyed the most singular protection of Divine Providence. This We believe must be attributed principally to the united, and therefore most efficacious, prayers, which, as of old for St. Peter, so now also for Ourselves, are constantly being poured forth by the Universal Church. Wherefore We first of all give profound thanks to God, the Giver of all good things, and we shall continue as long as life lasts to cherish in mind and heart gratitude for each and every favour. And next, there comes to Our mind the sweet remembrance of the motherly protection of the august Queen of Heaven; and this memory likewise We shall cherish and preserve inviolate, ever thanking her and proclaiming her benefits. From her, as from an abundant spring, are derived the streams of heavenly graces. "In her hand are the treasures of the mercies of the Lord." "God wisheth her to be the beginning of all good things." In the love of this tender mother, which We have constantly striven to cherish and to grow in day by day, We confidently hope that We may end Our life.

2. We have long desired to secure the welfare of the human race in an increase of devotion to the Blessed Virgin, as in a powerful citadel, and We have never ceased to encourage the constant use of the Rosary among Christians, by publishing every year since September 1, 1883, an Encyclical Letter on this subject, besides frequently issuing Decrees, as is well known. And now, since God in His merciful Providence has this year again allowed Us to see the approach of the month of October, which We have already consecrated to our Heavenly Queen under the title of the Rosary, We would not refrain from again addressing you; but summarizing in a few words all that we have hitherto done for the promotion of his form of prayer, We will crown our work by yet a new document, in which Our earnest desire

and zeal for this form of devotion to Mary may appear still more clearly, and the fervour of the faithful may be stimulated to the devout and constant use of this pious practice.

3. Impelled, therefore, by a constant desire that Christians should ever be convinced of the efficacy and dignity of the Rosary of Our Lady, We first of all pointed out that the origin of this form of prayer is divine rather than human, showing it to be an admirable garland woven from the Angelic Salutation, together with the Lord's Prayer, joined to meditation, and that this form of prayer was most powerful and particularly efficacious for attaining eternal life. For besides the special excellence of the prayers, it affords a powerful protection to faith and conspicuous models of virtue in the mysteries proposed for contemplation. We showed also how easy the devotion is and how suited to the people, offering an absolutely perfect model of domestic life in meditation on the Holy Family at Nazareth, and that therefore Christendom had never failed to experience its salutary effects.

4. For these reasons We have ever repeatedly encouraged the recitation of the Holy Rosary, and have endeavoured to increase its dignity by a more solemn cult, following in this the footsteps of our predecessors. Pope Sixtus V, of happy memory, approved the ancient custom of reciting the Rosary; Gregory XIII dedicated a day under this title, which Clement VIII afterwards inscribed in the martyrology, and Clement XI extended to the Universal Church. Benedict XIII inserted the feast in the Roman Breviary, and We, ourselves, in perpetual testimony of Our affection for this devotion commanded that the solemnity with its office should be celebrated in the Universal Church as a double of the second class, consecrating to this devotion the entire month of October. Finally we ordered the addition to the Litany of Loreto of the invocation "Queen of the most Holy Rosary," as an augury of victory in our present warfare.

5. It remains to be added that great value and utility accrue to the Rosary from the abundance of privileges and favours which adorn it, and more particularly from the rich treasures of indulgences attached to it. It is evident how greatly to the advantage of all who are solicitous for their eternal salvation is the obtaining of these benefits. For it is a question of obtaining either totally or partially a remission of the debt of temporal punishment which, even after guilt has been forgiven, must be paid either in this life or in the next. Vast indeed is the treasure won by the merits of Christ, His Mother and the Saints, to which our predecessor Clement VI. so aptly applied those words of the

Book of Wisdom: "She is an infinite treasure to men: which they that use become the friends of God." [74]

6. The Roman Pontiffs, making use of that supreme power granted them by God, have opened out the most abundant fountains of these graces to the members of the sodality of the Holy rosary and to those who recite the Rosary.

7. Wherefore, believing that the Crown of Mary will shine more brilliantly with these privileges and indulgences, as with an adornment of most precious gems, We have decided upon carrying out what We have long contemplated, namely, the publication of a "Constitution" concerning the rights, privileges and indulgences which are enjoyed by the members of the Rosary Sodality. This Our "Constitution" We intend to be a testimony of Our love to the most august Mother of God, and at the same time an encouragement to all the faithful and a reward of their piety, so that in the last hour of life they may be aided by her assistance and sweetly rest in her embrace. This blessing We heartily invoke from Almighty God through the Queen of the most Holy Rosary, and as an earnest and pledge of Divine Blessings, Venerable Brethren, to your clergy and to the people committed to your care, We gladly impart the Apostolic Benediction.

Given at St. Peter's, in Rome, on the 5th day of September, 1898, in the 21st year of Our Pontificate.

---

[74] Wisdom 7:14

For more wonderful
Traditional Catholic Books
Go to:

christthekinglibrary.com